WHAT ABOUT THE RUSSIANS—AND NUCLEAR WAR?

provides the essential background information about the Soviet Union and the U.S.-Soviet relationship for participation in Ground Zero's nationwide war/peace game—Firebreaks.

Threatened at her borders through the centuries, Russia has fought foreign invasion with an expansionist strategy. To understand Russia's development into a modern state is to gain an essential perspective on present Soviet nuclear policy, and how it affects us all.

Ground Zero is a nonpartisan educational organization dedicated to supplying information that the public has a right to know. Headed by Roger Molander, Ground Zero is headquartered in Washington, D.C. Mr. Molander served for seven years as a member of the National Security Council, spanning the administrations of presidents Nixon, Ford and Carter.

Earl Molander, a professor at Portland State University, is the Executive Director of the Ground Zero Pairing Project, linking U.S. and Soviet cities for people-to-people educational and cultural programs.

Books by GROUND ZERO

Nuclear War: What's in It for You?
What About the Russians—And Nuclear War?

Published by POCKET BOOKS

What About The Russians— and Nuclear War?

Ground Zero

PUBLISHED BY POCKET BOOKS NEW YORK

Another *Original* publication of POCKET BOOKS

POCKET BOOKS, a Simon & Schuster division of
GULF & WESTERN CORPORATION
1230 Avenue of the Americas, New York, N.Y. 10020

ISBN: 0-671-47209-7

First Pocket Books printing April, 1983

10 9 8 7 6 5 4 3 2 1

For all the people who type the words, wrap the bandages, stack the shelves, spin the records, teach the kids and keep the lights on, and deserve not to have to live with the threat of nuclear war

Contents

PART I
Condemned to Learning from History: The Russian and Soviet Past

PART II
Life Outside the Kremlin: Soviet Economy, Society and Culture

PART III
Shades of Totalitarianism:
How the Soviet Political System Works

PART IV
Beyond the Border Guards:
Soviet Foreign Policy and Actions in the
Postwar Era

PART V
Clash of the Titans:
The Soviet Military Challenge

PART VI
The Prospects for a Great Leap Forward:
The Future of U.S.-Soviet Relations

Foreword

"What about the Russians?" has long been a stock response to the notion that the United States set limits on its nuclear weapons program. Whether the proposals be for unilateral action or for bilateral action, as in the case of the nuclear weapons freeze proposals on so many ballots in legislative agendas in the early 1980s, the question is the same. In fact, it has been asked so frequently as to be almost a cliché. Cliché or not, it is an absolutely legitimate question.

The policies of the Soviet Union, whether we like them or not, are fundamental when we think about American security. For too long, those who have proposed curtailment of the U.S. weapons buildup by arms negotiations or other means have given too little thought to that basic question in the minds of so many Americans: "What about the Russians?"

For the great majority of the people asking this question, it is an honest one—they don't know what the Russians are doing and why, and they want an explanation. For others, however, this response has become a shield behind which they can avoid confronting the reality of 10,000 nuclear weapons pointed at the United States and their bewilderment to do something about it.

This book, then, is being written for the average American who has to go to the polls every other year and vote for candidates who will act as their agents in providing national security. It is also being written for those people who have argued that we have to do something about the nuclear war problem but don't know what. But above all it is our hope that this book will stimulate the essential debate we need in order to answer the question posed in the title.

The first book by Ground Zero, *Nuclear War: What's in It for You?*, sought to answer, without any political bias, questions that Americans have been asking for a long time about nuclear war. This book, an outgrowth of that volume and the experience of Ground Zero Week in April 1982, has also been written without a particular political perspective or point of view. The approach is consistent with the commitment of Ground Zero and the Ground Zero Pairing Project to provide the public with strictly nonpartisan, nonadvocacy educational materials and programs.

Winston Churchill once described the Soviet Union as "a riddle wrapped in mystery inside an enigma." Although the characterization is less true now, the Soviet Union is still a fundamentally different society from ours, one with a different history, culture, political system and economic system, and even different military doctrine and hardware. But if we are both to continue to occupy the same planet, we have no choice but to make the effort to understand our Soviet counterparts. Bear this in mind if you find yourself bogged down a bit in some of the long but important history of the Russian Empire, or in the Byzantine workings of the Soviet government, or in the subtle differences between U.S. and Soviet concepts of deterrence. Feel free to skip around a bit and read some of the less weighty material, such as descriptions of everyday life in the Soviet Union, or the rapid rise and demise of détente, or the character of the new Communist Party chief, Yuri Andropov. This book is not designed to give you a complete and perfect understanding of the Soviet Union (as if that were possible). But if it breaks down any of the barriers of ignorance and fear that keep these two great countries on the brink of destroying the world, then it has achieved its purpose.

As always, there are many people to whom a special debt is owed for their contributions to a sizeable undertaking such as this one. No fewer than sixty professional Sovietologists and national security experts, individuals whose expertise derives from their research as university faculty and from service within the government, contributed to the writing of this book. Among them, we would like to single out for a special expression of appreciation Dan Caldwell and Mark Garrison at the Center for Foreign Policy Development at Brown University, both of whom reviewed early drafts of the manuscript in its entirety (Dan having written one of the chapters); Walter Slocombe, Steve Hadley, Robert Legvold, Michael Carey and Barry Blechman, all of whom reviewed and provided comment on large segments of the book; and Pat Campbell of the Ground Zero staff, who wrote Chapters 5 and 6. Additional expressions of appreciation are due Marty Asher, editor-in-chief of Pocket Books, and Trish Todd, associate editor, for their support and assistance in the project; Marc Miller, for holding the writing team together; Richard Dennis, the Rockefeller Family Fund and the Scherman Fund for their financial support; and Lynn Hockaden, who typed and copyedited the entire manuscript many times over, and did so far more flawlessly than those who wrote it. Despite so heavy a debt to those who have assisted us, responsibility for the final product remains ours alone.

EARL A. MOLANDER
Executive Director
The Ground Zero Pairing Project

ROGER C. MOLANDER
Executive Director
Ground Zero

January 1983

PART I
Condemned to Learning from History:
The Russian and Soviet Past

Chapter 1

Mother Russia: The Roots of Soviet Politics and Power

"What about the Russians—and nuclear war?" is a redundancy. If it weren't for the fact that the Soviet Union has a nuclear arsenal capable of obliterating our society, most of us probably wouldn't give the Russians, their history, culture, political system, economic development or defense budget a second thought. But precisely because they *do* have those nuclear weapons, we as individuals and as a nation must concern ourselves with them. In this respect, such knowledge for Americans *is* power—power to understand the Russian factors in the historical equation that put us in the nuclear dilemma where we now find ourselves— and power to find our way out.

Stepping into the Russian Past

The Russian past has a direct bearing on contemporary Soviet society and the perspective of Soviet leaders on matters of national power and defense, and international relations and trust, matters that impinge directly on the U.S.-Soviet relationship and the threat of nuclear war. We see there the historical roots of the near-paranoia of contemporary Soviet leaders about U.S. nuclear weapons in Western Europe, their seeming obsession with assembling more and more nuclear weapons of their own, and their long-standing mistrust of U.S. motives in arms control and other peacemaking efforts. These are not the whole story, but they are the beginnings of the story. Churchill once spoke of the end of the beginning of World War II. Our purpose here is to outline what is hoped will be the beginning of the end of a World War III.

3

To review the history of Russia before the Russian Revolution and the formation of the Soviet state is to focus on what has undoubtedly been the essential obsession of Russian political leadership over its nearly 800-year history: the power and defense of Russia. This concern is rooted in the geography of the central Eurasian land mass that Russia occupies, and in the distinctive historical experience of the Russian people.

Taiga, Tundra, and Steppe: Soviet Geography

The country presently known as the Soviet Union, or Union of Soviet Socialist Republics (USSR), covers the vast central expanse of eastern Europe and Asia, close to one-fourth of the world's land area. Historically the country has been known as "Russia," a name that has persisted only outside the Soviet Union, after the official name change to "USSR" in 1922 (under the direct supervision of Joseph Stalin, Commissar of Nationalities). The persistence of the "Russia" identification is in part because the country's boundaries are not radically different from those of the Russian Empire at its zenith in 1917, and in part because the dominant national group, both in numbers and political power, is Russian by birth.

The land area of the present-day Soviet Union is almost two and one-half times that of the United States. The population in 1980 was 265 million, 40 million more than the United States. Although dominated by Russians (52 percent) and related Slavic groups, such as Ukrainians (16 percent) and Belorussians (4 percent), there is a sizeable minority population, especially in the south-central region, where Uzbeks, Kazakhs and other groups of the Moslem faith dominate. In total, there are some 180 different nationalities represented within the USSR, and about 125 native languages and dialects.

The majority of the Soviet land mass is at a latitude comparable to Canada, with a similar climate—long, cold winters and short summers. In addition, the physical characteristics of much of the Soviet landscape are as forbidding as its climate. There are prominent regions in the Soviet Union that are heavily mountainous, including the country's southern rim and the Pacific northeast. There is also an extensive desert in the south-central region east of the Caspian Sea.

But the dominant feature of the Soviet landscape is a vast plain that stretches from the country's European borders on the west to the Pacific coast on the east. This unhappy combination of soil and climate has given the USSR a tiny arable land area of no more than 10 percent of the total area of the country.

The Origins of Russia and Russian Orthodoxy

The people we know as the present-day Russians have a long and continuous history in the vast expanses of forest and steppe (a prairie region similar to that in the Great Plains of the United States) in what is the Soviet Union of today. The earliest ancestors of the *Rus,* as these people were known for centuries, were Salvic tribes whose presence in the area was recorded as early as the first century A.D. Eventually, the Slavs became divided into three general groupings: West Slavs (Poles, Czechs and Slovaks); South Slavs (Serbs, Croatians, Macedonians, Slovenes, Montenegrins and Bulgars); and East Slavs (Russians, Ukrainians and Belorussians). By the ninth century, the East Slavs had evolved into a grouping of city-states with extensive trading relationships with the surrounding areas. The term *Rus*—eventually "Russians"—came to be applied to the most powerful of the East Slavic groups, who came under the protection and control of a Viking warrior elite, the Varangians. The Varangian leader established his government in the city of Novgorod, but after his death his principal lieutenant moved the *Rus* capital to Kiev, where it developed into a major early medieval city of eastern Europe.

As the Kievan Russians developed their commercial enterprises and city, the ruling elite came under the influence of the Eastern Orthodox Church, which was based in Constantinople (present-day Istanbul). Through political controls and missionary activity, Eastern Orthodox Christianity became an important feature of life in the *Rus* cities, especially among the nobility. Eventually, Eastern Orthodoxy was assimilated and adopted by the bulk of the population and became an important element of national consciousness. This helped unite the Russian people with other Eastern Orthodox Christians to the south, while dividing them from Latin (Church of Rome) Christians in central and northern Europe, with whom they would often be at war.

Despite its commercial successes, Kiev eventually went into decline, in part because of continuous warfare with new nomadic tribes penetrating the southern steppes from Asia. In the thirteenth century, the most powerful of these tribes, the Mongols, swept into the area and were able to subdue the *Rus* principalities with relative ease, beginning a 200-year period of Mongol domination of *Rus* lands and people.

The Muscovite Tsars: Why Was Ivan So Terrible and Peter So Great?

In the years prior to the Mongol invasion, the northern city of Moscow (Muscovy) was a relatively minor Russian settlement. However, after the Mongol invasion and resultant decline of Kiev, Russian princes in Moscow were able to build a measure of strength and independence, although they were still required to make an annual journey to the south to pay the necessary taxes and tributes to the Mongol khan at the mouth of the Volga River.

Over a 250-year period, from the midthirteenth to midsixteenth centuries, the Muscovite princes gradually freed themselves from Mongol control and established a strong central government and bureaucracy. In the process, they brought under their control the other Russian principalities to the south, oversaw the beginnings of serfdom in the surrounding countryside and laid the foundations for an empire.

Whereas the pre-Mongol period had been relatively free of major warfare, the Mongol invasion and the rise of Muscovy represented a new period of intense warfare and destruction in eastern Europe, which created the conditions for a Muscovite warfare state. Muscovy was a warfare state in the sense that the leadership of the state was primarily concerned with war, and the resources of the population were subordinated to the needs of warfare and the state. Christianity, too, was mobilized to an alliance with the Muscovite state in its wars against the "infidel" Tartars, as the occupying Mongol tribes were known.

During this early period, Muscovy was ruled by a succession of princes who took the title of "tsar" as part of their effort to replace Mongol imperial dominance, in fact and in theory. (*Tsar*, like *Kaiser*, is a derivative of *Caesar*, and was chosen to imply Caesar-like regal legitimacy.) Among the more notable of this early line of tsars was Ivan IV, who in the sixteenth century defeated the Mongol khanates of Kazan and Astrakhan.

Ivan IV ruled as an all-powerful autocrat, a position he maintained with the 6,000-man *oprichniki,* who dressed completely in black and affected highly conspicuous symbols as they terrorized the countryside to establish tsarist absolutism. Ironically, it was not these activities that earned him the nickname "Ivan the Terrible"; the characterization was given as a compliment by a contemporary, meaning terrible or threatening to the enemies of Russia. For this he is considered a great national hero.

Ivan the Terrible ended the Varangian line by killing his own son. Russia entered the seventeenth century with a brief but important period, known as the "Time of Troubles," in which Poland sought to establish dynastic control over the Muscovite state. During this time the land was torn with civil war, including the first great revolt of the common people, and the Polish armies occupied Moscow. This period ended in 1613 when the first of the Romanov family became tsar and defeated the Polish enemies. The first Romanovs also established serfdom on a permanent, legal foundation and subordinated the church to the state. By the middle of the century the new dynasty had gained many territories in Europe and northern Asia.

Near the end of that century perhaps the greatest of all Romanov tsars, appropriately known as "Peter the Great," ascended the throne. Peter ruled Russia from 1689 to 1725, a period in which he transformed a backward but enormously large and potentially resourceful state into a powerful empire at last linked with the far more advanced countries of central and western Europe. From his boyhood onward, Peter was fascinated with everything European—boats, military organization, weaponry, culture and social organization. Once mature—he had ascended the throne initially at the age of ten under his half-sister as regent—he set upon a program of modernizing the Russian army. He established a system of rank in the military and civil service that was based on ability, not heredity, although these professions remained closed to the bulk of the population. These military reforms, spurred on by wars with a new enemy, Sweden, stimulated reforms in other areas, directed at Westernization of the country. However, Peter did nothing to improve the conditions of the Russian peasants, whose serfdom was little different from slavery. His ruthless exploitation of the rural population—heavy taxation, a census that classified many previously free peasants as serfs, and forced recruitment into the army—led to the second of the major peasant revolts.

Peter's espousal of Westernization in defiance of old orthodox tradition was widely resisted by important elements of Russian society, including his own son, who was either killed by Peter or allowed to die in prison. As a result, Peter was followed by a series of weak rulers until the ascendance of Catherine the Great in 1762.

Catherine's 34-year rule was marked by the continuation of the expansionist tendencies of her predecessors and Russia became a significant force in European politics. She instituted a number of administrative reforms, but did nothing to improve the lot of the serfs. As a result, Catherine's reign was the setting for one of the most famous Russian rebellions, under the leadership of a Cossack named Pugachev. The response of Catherine and her successors was not the much-needed reforms in serfdom, but further repression of the peasant population.

The Nineteenth Century: Roots of the Russian Revolution

The nineteenth century in Russia opened with Alexander I on the throne. His reign was characterized by some moderate reforms in the bureaucracy and the educational system but no major changes in the conditions of the serfs. Alexander's reign is best known as the period in which Napoleon made his ill-fated march across Russia, only to fall victim to the cruelties of the Russian winter and the tenacious Russian defense of the motherland. The story has been memorialized in Leo Tolstoy's epic novel, *War and Peace* and in Tchaikovsky's *1812* Overture. With the defeat of Napoleon, Russia became the dominant land power in Europe.

Following Alexander's sudden death in 1825, the Decembrist uprising, a military revolt among certain regiments whose officers sought to impose Western constitutional reform on the Russian political system, took place. Although the Decembrist uprising failed, it became an important symbol of the potential for revolution among the generations of Russian radicals and revolutionaries that followed in the nineteenth century. It also terrified Alexander's successors, who saw in the Decembrist uprising the seeds of Russia's destruction. As a result, the tsars of nineteenth-century Russia tempered government involvement in political reform with increased efforts to control both popular unrest and radicalization, never certain which would offer greater security to their throne.

Notable among these later tsars was Alexander II, whose reign began with defeat by Britain in the Crimean War. Alexander saw serfdom as an expensive and inefficient vestige of Russia's past and freed the 25 million Russian serfs by imperial proclamation in 1861. (Abraham Lincoln's Emancipation Proclamation, signed in 1863, freed the slaves in the United States at almost the same time.) He also continued the expansion of the Russian empire eastward into central Asia, where Russian and British forces came closer to one another, then withdrew, leaving Afghanistan as the "neutral buffer" (for 100 years, until 1979). When he died in 1881, the victim of a terrorist bomb, Russia controlled close to 8,000,000 square miles of eastern Europe and Asia, almost the area it controls today. It was some 13,000 times larger than the 600-square-mile area the principality of Muscovy encompassed in the fourteenth century.

The reaction to Alexander's assassination was the reinforcement of the absolutist state, which continued to tolerate a modest degree of political involvement of urban estates and nobility in local affairs. Ironically, the day of his assassination he had signed a decree creating a new consultative assembly for Russia. His successor, the reactionary Alexander III, promptly cancelled the decree.

The sudden introduction into Russia of the forces of the Industrial Revolution, a social transformation that had been underway in western Europe and America for some time, led to substantial social mobility and indirectly to improvements in the standard of living. It carried with it all of the wretched evils of the experience—a peasant class forced into the cities to live in urban slums and struggle for employment and subsistence.

Industrial development was characterized by the acceptance of a dominant role for the state in the development of the economy. A high premium was placed on those enterprises that fostered an increase in national power and a low premium on those that improved the standard of living. It also brought an acute sense of inferiority over the fact that Russia lacked the capabilities of Western societies and desperately needed to match them or suffer the consequences.

The final phase of the prerevolutionary period in Russia saw the country under the control of Tsar Nicholas II, an individual of little personal strength and character. His political ambitions led him to refuse negotiations with the Japanese for spheres of influence in East Asia, where he sought to extend Russian control over Manchuria and Korea, thus provoking a disastrous war with Japan. The resulting hardship at home precipitated the Revolution of 1905, the bellwether of the Russian Revolution of 1917, which would overthrow the monarchy and end 400 years of tsarist rule.

Weighing the Baggage of the Past

At the beginning of the twentieth century Americans were celebrating three hundred years of an open and democratic political tradition, offering substantial political and economic freedom to virtually all its citizens. From the beginning, we were a robust country, brimming with self-confidence yet not greatly concerned about our needs for national defense or our place relative to the longtime powers of Western civilization in Europe. As a nation, the U.S. knew little or nothing of Russia's foreign invasions, autocratic political traditions or feelings of inferiority. As individuals, the majority of Americans knew even less of exploitation, terror and communal life. This historical innocence would substantially influence the posture of this country when World War I forced it to the center of the world stage, where it would play a dominant role through most of the century.

Halfway around the globe, Russia also entered the twentieth century, but with a far blacker history behind it. The modern-day Soviet state carries much of its history with it as it forms its policies in the international arena. The frequent invasions have created an obsession about security on its borders. The response has been expansion into adjacent areas where possible, epitomized in the Soviet determination to retain its buffer of Eastern European satellite states and its near-paranoia at the prospect of Western European deployment of cruise and Pershing II missiles, which could overfly those borders with ease. Furthermore, Russian de-

fenses have always seemed oriented toward surpassing suffi-
ciency, whether it be in the nineteenth century, when the
tsars maintained the largest land force in Europe, or the
contemporary era, when the Soviet military and political
leaders continue to press for more and more nuclear weapons as security against the threat from the U.S. and its allies.

Chapter 2

The Russian Revolution: What They Revere and We Fear

From the Soviet perspective, the Russian Revolution is proof positive of what is possible under the guiding wisdom of Marx and Lenin. As such, each year the anniversary of the Revolution is an occasion for massive parades and speeches of considerable energy, filled with praise for the virtues of the hammer and sickle of Communist society and saber-rattling promises of instant retaliation against any who might threaten it.

For many Americans, the Revolution was the first "Communist takeover," masterminded by a ruthless cadre of dedicated revolutionists driven by an all-encompassing anti-capitalist and anti-democratic ideology.

Americans fear that the Russian Revolution could be repeated elsewhere in the world and ultimately, in our worst nightmare, in the U.S. itself. In fact, at two times in this century—just after World War I and again in the early 1950s—we gave serious thought as to whether it might not in fact be a prospect for our own country. Our reactions were visceral, seeking to purge those tainted with this alien ideology from our government, schools and media.

The Ideological Underpinnings of Revolution: Marxism and Leninism

In 1848, as the United States embarked on the path to building what eventually would become the largest capitalist economy in the world, an expatriate German radical, Karl Marx, with the assistance of an English industrialist, Friedrich Engels, published in London a short, 40-page pam-

12

phlet entitled *The Communist Manifesto,* attacking directly the evils of the capitalist system and appealing for a violent revolution of the oppressed working class: "The proletarians have nothing to lose but their chains. They have a world to win. Working men of the world, unite!" Later, Marx published *Das Kapital,* a long and turgid analysis of capitalism that eventually became the bible of socialists everywhere.

Ironically, when Marx's dream of the overthrow of capitalism did in fact occur in a European country, it was in the country both Marx and Engels initially felt would be the least likely candidate—Russia, which had not yet passed through capitalism, a necessary and inevitable stage en route to socialism.

Yet there were characteristics of Russian society—in particular the exploitation of the serfs and a radical political tradition—that ultimately would provide the essential constituent elements of revolution.

Among the radical intellectuals of late nineteenth-century Russia with a particular bent toward Marxist thought and action was a young man named Vladimir Ilyich Ulyanov, an ardent revolutionary who eventually took a false name— Lenin. In 1900, Lenin, having been first imprisoned and then exiled for his radical activities, was living in Germany, where he expanded his efforts to adapt Marxist thought on politics and revolution to the unique situation of tsarist Russia in the early twentieth century. In 1902, he published *Chto Delat?* (What Is to Be Done?), the first extensive statement of the political ideology known as "Leninism" that he would use to create the Bolshevik revolution and found the Soviet state.

In their 1903 Congress in London, the organization of Russian Marxist socialists known as the Russian Social Democratic Labor Party, of which Lenin was a member, split into two factions. The Bolsheviks, led by Lenin, felt the Party should remain a small, tightly disciplined group of professional revolutionaries capable of maintaining the secrecy and strict discipline which could lead the workers (and even peasants) toward revolution. The Mensheviks sought a broader base in the working class and intelligentsia.

In January 1905, a peaceful demonstration outside the tsar's palace in St. Petersburg by workers and others protesting the deprivations brought about the the Russo-Japanese war was fired upon by tsarist troups, killing about 200 people. News of the needless killing on "Bloody Sunday," as it was called, provoked riots and strikes throughout European Russia. October 1905 saw the creation of the St. Petersburg Soviet of Workers' and Soldiers' Deputies, an ad hoc council of elected representatives set up by the socialists to give direction to the workers' protest movement.

The uprising demonstrated to Lenin and other revolutionaries that the potential for revolution in tsarist Russia lay very close to the surface.

In August of 1914, the outbreak of World War I placed socialists everywhere in a difficult position: workers in each country were fighting other workers. Lenin urged his comrades in Russia and abroad to turn the "imperialist war," as he called it, into a "revolutionary war," which would overthrow the capitalist governments and their backers, whom he held responsible for the conflict. At first his views commanded little support, as they seemed too extreme, but by 1916, Russia was counting her loss of young men in the millions and the taste for war on the front and back home was waning. The frustration and anger of the Russian people (including many people in the government and wealthier classes) toward Tsar Nicholas II and his incompetent administration was heightened by rumors about an intrigue involving the "holy man" Rasputin, a mystic monk, who many felt had mesmerized the Tsarina Alexandra.

Despite the storm warning on the domestic horizon, when the Russian Revolution actually did begin on March 8, 1917, the speed and extent with which it engulfed the country surprised even the most optimistic of the revolutionaries, not to mention the privileged classes. In less than a week, the 400-year-old tsarist dynasty was toppled and a new democratic provisional government had taken its place.

The Russian Revolution: On the Streets and in the Battlefield

The Russian Revolution had two relatively distinct phases. The first phase began on March 8, 1917 with strikes for higher wages in the capital city of Petrograd (the name had been changed because St. Petersburg sounded too German; it is now Leningrad). The strike spread rapidly throughout the city, and attempts by the tsarist government and troops to reassert control failed.

Under pressure from the mobs in the streets, various political factions in the *Duma,* the representative (but largely ineffectual) legislative assembly convened by Tsar Nicholas after the 1905 revolt, met. On March 12, after much debate, it set up a provisional committee to direct the country. The tsar had no alternative but to abdicate, and as no other member of his family would take his place, the monarchy collapsed with him. On March 15, the provisional committee was formed into a Provisional Government. The government was not the only force on the scene, however, as a new "soviet," similar to the 1905 workers' council, had already been formed, including Socialist deputies from the *Duma,* representatives of the striking workers' committees, leaders of various left-wing political organizations and mutinous military units.

Within the first month of its existence, the impotence of the Provisional Government was demonstrated in the growing conflict over whether Russia should prolong her participation in the war or conclude peace as quickly as possible on terms whereby none of the belligerents annexed territory or paid war indemnities. Aware of these divisions, the German government sent a special train from Switzerland across Germany to Russia carrying Lenin and other Russian political émigrés known to oppose continued Russian participation in the war. Lenin and his supporters promptly set about the task of expanding Bolshevik influence in the new system of soviets[1] or local councils, which by now were forming all over the country.

Lenin was forced into hiding and Leon Trotsky, another leading radical who had recently joined the Bolsheviks, was arrested. In mid-July, the Provisional Government, which had been joined by the moderate socialists, collapsed, and Alexander Kerensky, who was a member of both the national Soviet and *Duma,* became prime minister. His government, opposed both from the left and from the right, proved as impotent as the preceding one. Seeing their opportunity,

---

[1]Note the distinction between these local "soviets" and the national "Soviet" formed in March of 1917.

on October 22, the central committee of the Bolshevik Party voted in favor of an armed insurrection as Trotsky, released from jail, rallied opinion in the soviets and skillfully undermined the government's prestige.

The October Revolution

Lenin's partisans, who had the backing of soldiers and Red Guards, had little difficulty in winning control of the capital. From this position, they declared the system of local soviets to be the single legitimate source of power in the country, thereby circumventing the national Soviet, where they did not have a majority. When the national Soviet did meet, non-Bolshevik members of the local soviets withdrew from the Congress in protest against the Bolsheviks' unconstitutional methods. On November 8, in their absence, the Congress voted in favor of a new government with Lenin as premier and Trotsky as commissar of foreign affairs. At long last, Lenin and his Bolshevik followers were in power.

Under the watchword "All power to the soviets," similar uprisings all across Russia brought local soviets, many controlled by the Bolsheviks, to power. In fact, in a nation whose earlier social and political structure had now almost completely disintegrated, the soviets were the strongest political force. By the end of November, Bolshevik-controlled soviets were in power throughout most of the country.

Immediately upon gaining power, the Bolshevik government began a campaign to take Russia out of the war. The Treaty of Brest-Litovsk, signed in March 1918, ceded to Germany the territories its armies occupied, plus the rest of the Baltic region (the future states of Lithuania, Latvia and Estonia), Finland, and even the Ukraine in the south, which had rich food resources and had been a separate national entity until its annexation by Russia in 1654.

The treaty cost Russia enormous territorial losses, undoing three centuries of Russian expansion. She lost one-third of her population, one-third of her cultivatable land and one-half of her heavy industry. But the Bolsheviks had not been forced to give up any native Russian areas, and the treaty gave them breathing space to build the Red Army and consolidate their power at home. There they were confronted with a civil war, from elements on the right—the

"White Armies" plus middle-class elements opposed to socialism, and even some fellow socialists.

Civil War

In the Civil War, the Bolsheviks had strength in the cities and some important allies, including the more "radical" Socialist Revolutionaries. On the other hand, some of the strongest opposition to Bolshevik rule came from the "mainline" Socialist Revolutionaries, who had strong support in the villages. The peasants had seized the land for themselves and wanted to keep control of it. But the cities were starving and the Bolsheviks introduced a desperate policy of ruthlessly requisitioning peasant food stocks. The mainline Socialist Revolutionaries were able to form a rival government in the Volga region during the summer of 1918, but it soon collapsed, as the moderates were caught between two stronger opposing forces: the "Reds" and the "Whites."[2]

The Red Army, with Trotsky as People's Commissar for War, soon became a fairly well-disciplined and well-equipped force, more than a match for its opponents. The Red soldiers felt they were fighting for a noble and progressive cause, whereas morale was more tenuous among the Whites.

Allied Intervention

In April of 1918, the Allies, anxious to restore the eastern front and fearful that supplies sent to the Russians during the war would end up in German hands, landed troops in Russia. The Japanese supplied large contingents in the east, but there were only a few thousand English and French and also some Americans.

The intervention proved insufficient to topple the Bolshevik government, however, and as the Whites were pushed back both in Siberia and in southern Russia (in Ukraine) during 1919, the withdrawal of Allied troops speedily fol-

---

[2]The degree of political factionation in this period was considerable. On the right there were elements of the old tsarist aristocracy, governmental bureaucracy and officer corps. The left included the Bolsheviks, the left-of-center supporters of Kerensky and mainline and radical Socialist Revolutionaries.

lowed, leaving much bitterness against the foreigners who had intervened.

By November 1920 the civil war was over and nearly all the former Russian empire was in the hands of the Bolsheviks. The civil war had taken an enormous toll on the country, especially in terms of casualties from famine and disease, and the scars remained for many years. The rural areas were particularly hard hit; the market for food had collapsed with the policy of forced acquisition of food grains and livestock from the farmers, and there was little incentive to produce a surplus to sell. As a result, in 1921, the grain crop in Russia was only 40 percent of the 1900–1913 average. The Bolsheviks responded by abandoning the state monopoly on grain and reverting to a mixed economy under the "New Economic Policy," but the beneficial results of this switch did not show themselves immediately. When famine accompanied by severe drought in the summer of 1922 ruined the spring-sown grain, response came from the American Relief Administration (ARA), which had been providing American foodstuffs to Belgium and France during the war and afterward to the countries of central and eastern Europe, together with European relief organizations and the League of Nations. By March 1922 the ARA was providing food for some 10 million Russians.[3]

The "Communist Threat" in Action

The period of the Russian Revolution demonstrated Lenin's political mastery, first as he maneuvered for power within the ranks of the Russian socialist movement, then within the soviets and finally against domestic and international forces that sought to remove the Bolsheviks from power. Together with his Bolshevik followers, Lenin's survival and triumph were remarkable, beginning as a minority faction, seizing and protecting this power from democratic forces and then maintaining a regime surrounded by hostile forces who refused to recognize its legitimacy. It was a feat accomplished through cold-blooded pragmatism unfettered by ideology, always buying time, as in the Treaty of Brest-Litovsk, always seeking to undermine relations between its

---

[3]At the 1972 summit meeting, Soviet leader Alexei Kosygin commented to President Nixon that he would never forget the aid his village received from the U.S.

adversaries and foreign governments. It was everything that contemporary Soviet leaders praise and their American counterparts fear.

The struggle was not without its price, however. The four years of strife between 1917 and 1921, in particular the program of "war communism" and its total mobilization of the country's human and material resources to wage war and maintain Bolshevik power, snuffed out the last traces of social democratic ideals among the Bolshevik movement's early supporters. Although it sealed the fate of a despotic tsarist aristocracy, it helped pave the way for Stalin and totalitarianism and demonstrated for many Americans the inherent evils in the Communist-inspired and Communist-assisted revolutions that followed elsewhere in the world.

Chapter 3

Building and Protecting Soviet Socialism: The Stalin Era

Joseph Stalin. "Uncle Joe." Thirty years after his death Soviet politics and society and U.S.-Soviet relations still reverberate from his rule. Born Iosif Dzhugashvili, Stalin was the personification of the revolutionary name he chose for himself—"man of steel." He was also the embodiment of the determination of the Soviet Bolsheviks to preserve and expand the achievements of their revolution through enormous sacrifices of life and material well-being, sacrifices which the Soviet people, under whatever motivation, ultimately did make.

When Lenin died in 1924, Stalin assumed control of the Party, invoking a manner or rule true to his chosen name. From this position, he combined the traditional nationalism and authoritarian heritage of the tsarist era with Lenin's revolutionary spirit to build a powerful, industrial, socialist state. To make the achievements of his long rule possible, he inaugurated a brutal program of industrialization and collectivization that transformed the country from an agricultural to an industrial society. As he consolidated his power, he instituted a "Stalinist" personality cult and a system of mass terror highlighted by massive purges of the Party, military and government in the mid- and late-1930s.

Stalin was the consummate dictator, his political system so total in its control of the public and private lives of its citizens that it gave rise to a new word in the lexicon of politics—"totalitarianism." Whatever its critics might say, however, the totalitarian Soviet state played a key role in the Allied defeat of Nazi Germany in World War II and since then has challenged the U.S. for global supremacy in the postwar era.

The New Economic Plan

The New Economic Policy (NEP), which Lenin instituted in the spring of 1921 was in sharp contrast to the "war communism" of the previous three years, which was a program of centralized governmental control of virtually every aspect of economic life. Many of Lenin's Bolshevik followers believed war communism was the appropriate structure for the new socialist state; nevertheless, Lenin felt that the state did not have the resources to undertake the rebuilding of the country which all recognized was necessary, and he was able to pursuade his critics to support the NEP.

The NEP permitted freedom of trading within the country and piece-rate and overtime payments to workers, promoted overseas investment in Russia by foreign capitalists and recognized the rights of private property, which had been suspended under war communism. The industrial sector was controlled by economic councils that had both governmental and industrial representation. With the reestablishment of a state banking system, profit-and-loss accounting in the industrial sector and cash wages and graduated rents, the economic system under the NEP, according to some Communist critics, began to look a great deal like a variation on capitalism. Regardless, the NEP was successful in its short-term goals, with production and trade approaching pre-war levels, the currency stable and the agricultural sector once again producing adequate yields by the end of 1924.

The Death of Lenin and the Rise of Stalin

The death of Lenin on January 21, 1924, after a two-year illness, precipitated a power struggle within the Bolshevik ranks. In this struggle, Trotsky, Lenin's most famous colleague, was overcome by an alliance between Stalin, then head of the general secretary of the Communist Party, and two of the leading conservative Bolsheviks, Kamenev and Zinoviev.

In August 1924, having observed the failure of the Bolshevik hope for world revolution, Stalin suggested that from then on the Soviet Union should pursue "socialism in one country," i.e., that the Communist revolution in Russia would focus first and foremost on developing a socialist state in the home country as a precondition to international socialist revolution. This position was in sharp contrast to the internationalism of other Bolsheviks who had seen their role as leading a worldwide Communist movement through the Communist International (Comintern), an organizational vehicle founded for this purpose by Lenin in 1919.

With the abandonment of the Comintern's thrust toward international revolution and the turn inward of the Soviet economy, Russia began to reestablish the separation and isolation from Europe that had characterized the tsarist era and that would be, with the partial exception of the 1941-45 period, the model of Soviet relationships with the West to the present day. Although the Comintern was an impediment to improved relations between the new Soviet government and other European governments, formal diplomatic relations were established with the majority of them by 1924 (recognition by the U.S. did not come until 1933).

Stalin was able to quickly consolidate his power, although he still had to contend with Trotsky and other more dogmatic Communists who felt the revolution was being betrayed by Stalin's narrow Russian focus, and by an economic system—the NEP—that was undermining its own socialist base. Trotsky was rapidly being demoted from positions of authority, finally being exiled from the country in 1929. He lived in Turkey, Norway and finally Mexico City, where he was axed to death in 1940 by an attacker many assume was a Stalinist agent.

Collectivization and Industrialization

Although the Bolsheviks had always been a Party that emphasized modernization and industrialization, Stalin proposed a two-pronged program in 1928 for the massive industrialization of the Soviet economy and the collectivization of agriculture under state control. He proclaimed that he would build socialism with "the methods employed by the Pharaohs for building the pyramids." He was motivated in part by a desire to shift back towards socialism and away from the NEP and in part by his belief that the Soviet Union could not withstand an invasion from Great Britain, Germany or any other advanced industrial country with a far larger industrial base. Stalin announced, "We are fifty to one hundred years behind the advanced countries. We must make good this lag in ten years. Either we do it or they crush us."

Industrialization on the scale envisioned by Stalin required major social dislocations. To begin, there was a massive shift of capital away from the consumer-goods sector to heavy industry, in particular those sectors of heavy industry essential for defense. This shift would be accompanied by a shift of labor in the same direction, much of it from the farm sector, which was targeted for intensive mechanization. The program also included a system of incentives for the most productive workers, technicians and industrial managers, which led to the growth of considerable differences in the economic welfare of the technical/managerial and working classes.

To feed the rapidly growing urban labor force, Stalin viciously enforced collectivization on the rural peasant population. In the process of suppressing the peasant resistance to this move, many *kulaks,* the richest of the peasants, were deported and resettled in distant areas, primarily near new industrial sites, and some were sent to Siberian labor camps. The result was a highly unproductive period of Soviet agriculture and the death of as many as 3 million peasants in the resulting famines of 1931 and 1932.

By this time, the revolutionary enthusiasm for the First Five-Year Plan (which had lasted for only three and a half years) had given way to a more sober and realistic process in the Second Five-Year Plan. In a sense, industrial expansion was being "derevolutionized" and becoming more characteristic of rapid industrialization in other countries.

The Purges

In 1935, at the height of the drive for industrialization, Stalin began a massive purge of "old Bolsheviks" in the government and Party—those who had participated in the revolution—and the upper echelons of the army. The result was the elimination of any element of the society that might have been able to depose him in a national crisis, including his heir-apparent, Kirov, and the final consolidation of Stalin's power.

The numbers of people killed in the purges have been estimated in the millions, and the upper ranks of the Party, government, army and industrial bureaucracy were decimated. In the army alone, 3 of the 5 marshals of the Soviet Union, 13 of 15 army commanders, 30 of 58 corps commanders, 110 of 185 divisional commanders and 311 of 406 regimental commanders were purged.

Together with the anti-capitalist, anti-religious rhetoric of Marxism and the avowed revolutionary goals of the Comintern, the purges established an image in the minds of the people and leaders of Western Europe and America of a totalitarian Soviet state under the control of a ruthless Stalinist dictatorship hostile to a free democratic society.

1938: Looking Backward

Despite its accompanying social dislocations, the statistics on the Soviet industrial drive in the first two five-year plans are particularly impressive. According to one estimate, from 1928 to 1938, production of coal went up 274 percent, petroleum 133 percent, electric power 540 percent, and steel 318 percent. Compared to 1913, the overall level of industrial production in 1938 was up 800 percent. Equally important, by 1938 the production of grain and other agricultural products had recovered from the disastrous short-run effects of collectivization and reached 1928 and prewar levels. The consumer goods sector, however, was far behind these other areas, much as it is in the Soviet Union today.

However brutal and costly Stalin's forced industrialization and collectivization was, it did answer his critics' charges that he was not promoting a socialist state. More importantly, however, it demonstrated the foresight in Stalin's earlier warning about the need for military preparedness against a potential threat from the advanced industrialized West, a threat that was now presenting itself in the rise of Nazi Germany. Conscious of the German threat, Stalin continued to spur industrial expansion, even as he turned to diplomatic means to try to stave off an invasion of the Russian homeland.

With Friends Like These . . . : The
Diplomatic Search for Security

Before Hitler came to power in Germany in 1933, relations between the German and Soviet governments had been cordial for over a decade, dating to secret elements in the Treaty of Rapallo (1922), which permitted the German military to establish military bases and build defense plants in Russia (something they were forbidden by their surrender at Versailles) in exchange for German military training of the Red Army in modern warfare and a Russian share of defense production. As the Nazi regime began to show signs of being an openly militaristic, expansionist and anti-Communist regime, Soviet foreign policy shifted to form alliances with France and Czechoslovakia, and nonaggression pacts were made with neighboring Poland, Finland and the Baltic states on Russia's northwestern front. In 1934, the Soviet Union also joined the League of Nations, the same year that Germany withdrew. In keeping with this shift in relations, and with the obvious purpose of affecting public opinion abroad, the Comintern modified its program to reduce its call for revolution in the capitalist countries and instead sought alliances with indigenous socialist, liberal and radical parties and provided substantial, but unsuccessful, military assistance to the partisan Republicans in the Spanish Civil War.

In 1938, Stalin, still pursuing alliances, made secret overtures to the French and British governments to form a united front against German expansionist aims, but these efforts were rebuffed when Britain and Germany signed the now-infamous Munich pact. In 1939, Lityinov, the Soviet foreign minister, again proposed an Anglo-Franco-Soviet collective security agreement. The French were receptive, but the British government under Chamberlain stalled with complex formulae that required Soviet guarantees to countries that had not even sought them. Stalin then replaced Litvinov, who had been openly reviled by the Nazi government as a Jew, with Molotov. Three months later, on August 23, 1939, Stalin signed a mutual nonaggression pact with Germany.

The threat of a Russian front now behind him, Hitler invaded Poland on September 1, 1939. As the German *Blitzkrieg* stormed across Poland on September 17, 1939, Soviet troops, in keeping with a secret protocol in the nonaggression pact that partitioned Europe from the Arctic Ocean to the Black Sea, invaded Poland from the east on the pretext of protecting Soviet populations in Western Belorussia and the Ukraine. The partition of Poland was followed by the Soviet invasion of Finland on November 30, 1939. In the summer of 1940 the Baltic states (Estonia, Latvia and Lithuania), which had six months previously permitted Russian troops to enter their countries as part of the earlier mutual aid treaties with the Soviet government, were annexed to the Soviet Union and organized as soviet republics within the USSR.

By the end of June 1940, Norway, Denmark, the Netherlands, Belgium and France had fallen to the German *Blitzkrieg,* leaving Great Britain, which had joined the war with the Polish invasion and whose army had barely escaped at Dunkirk, standing alone against Hitler. These spectacular German successes in the first year of the war frightened Stalin, even though he had also made territorial advances, including the invasion of Romania in June 1940. He dispatched Molotov to Berlin in November of 1940 in hopes of striking a more secure agreement with the Nazi government. Molotov was unable to secure the guarantees that Stalin sought, however, and Soviet-German relations began to strain. Now uncertain of the future of the nonaggression treaty, Stalin pushed even harder for the buildup of the defense industries. In addition, he took his first formal position in the Soviet government, that of premier.

On the Eastern Front: "The Great Patriotic War"

Despite Stalin's reservations and fears about German intentions, and British warnings that the Germans could be preparing to invade Russia, "Operation Barbarossa," the German invasion of Russia that began on June 22, 1941, by his own admission took Stalin largely by surprise. In fact, some historians believe Stalin suffered some sort of breakdown, since it was left to Molotov to announce the invasion to the Russian people. After a week had passed, Stalin emerged from his Kremlin isolation to announce formation of a state defense committee with himself as chairman and to make his famous call to the Soviet people to "scorch the earth" before the invaders.

In the first five months of the German offensive, large areas of western and southern Russia were lost to the invading Nazi armies. By November, some 500,000 square miles of former Russian territory—an area nearly the size of that part of the United States east of the Mississippi River—was under German control. Leningrad was encircled (eventually close to 1,000,000 Russians died there in a 900-day siege) and the German army was 30 miles from Moscow.

With the German invasion of Russia, the complexion of relations between Russia and Great Britain, the only remaining combatant against Germany, changed. On the evening of June 22, 1941, Winston Churchill, who had become Prime Minister in May 1940 after public confidence in the Chamberlain government had waned, offered an alliance to Stalin with these words:

> . . . any man or state who fights on against Nazidom will have our aid. Any man who marches with Hitler is our foe . . . It follows, therefore, that we shall give whatever help we can to Russia and the Russian people.

Despite these promising words, British assistance was limited considerably by its own war needs. As British assistance began to trickle into Russia, a second event brought a dramatic change in the complexion of the war on the Russian front: on December 7, 1941, Japan attacked the U.S. naval base at Pearl Harbor. Within a week, the United States had declared war on Japan, and Germany had declared war on the United States. Suddenly, the Big Three—Great Britain, the Soviet Union and the United States—were allies against Germany, Japan, Italy and the other Axis powers.

Under pressure from the German invasion, the Russian army was forced to withdraw to the east. Large amounts of heavy industry, especially those machines needed for defense production, were moved east of Moscow to the Ural Mountain areas, and factories and machinery that could not be moved were destroyed. Within a few months, the factories were able to begin to manufacture the munitions and matériel necessary to sustain resistance to the German offensive.[1]

---

[1] Over 1,360 factories and about 10,000,000 people were evacuated during this period. Recovery was so rapid that in the second half of 1942, Soviet industry turned out 15,800 aircraft and 13,600 tanks, as well as 15,000 artillery pieces.

Over the next two years, from the spring of 1942 to the Allied invasion at Normandy in June 1944, the Red Army gradually pushed the German *Wehrmacht* west out of Russia. With the Normandy invasion, Stalin at last had the second front he had long sought, and long been promised, by the other Allied governments. By March 1945, the German defenses on both the eastern and western fronts had largely collapsed and the Allied forces were driving toward Berlin. Within a matter of weeks, the Red Army had completely surrounded Berlin, linked up with the British and American forces on the Elbe, sixty miles to the west. Shortly afterward, Hitler committed suicide and the German army surrendered. The hot war in Europe was over.

The (Not So) Grand Alliance

With the German attack on Russia in the summer of 1941, the "agreement for a joint action" had led the British to begin sending supplies and war matériel to their new ally and Stalin to expect that very soon a second front in the west would be launched. The alliance agreement had not specifically called for a second front, only for provision of support and assistance and the prohibition of any attempt at a separate peace with Germany by either side, and Stalin's request was refused. After the United States joined the war effort to form the "Grand Alliance," Stalin continued to insist that promises had been made by the allies for a second front and that he expected the front if not in 1942 then assuredly in the spring of 1943. Roosevelt's claim that the Anglo-American landing in North Africa represented "an effective second front" was rejected by Stalin, who was then given indications by Churchill that the front would come in August 1943, conditional on the enemy first being severely weakened. When the front finally did come in June 1944, it was followed, rather ironically, by an Anglo-American request that the Russian army accelerate its operations on the eastern front in order to relieve the German pressure in the west. Stalin complied.

Other factors that ate away at the Alliance were the "Polish question," revolving around post-war Soviet-Polish borders and which Polish government-in-exile (there was one in London and one in Moscow) would rule in the post-war period; the failure of Britain and the United States to consult Stalin on the terms of surrender to be imposed on Italy when it surrendered in 1943; the question of whether Germany would be partitioned at the war's conclusion; and the Red Army's movement into the Balkan states, including Romania and Bulgaria, thereby increasing the probability of Soviet domination of that region after the war.

Despite these problems, there were numerous cooperative efforts—the U.S. Army Air Force was permitted to use Soviet bases for shuttle bombing runs over Germany—and substantial aid to the Soviet Union for its part of the war effort from both the United States and Britain. According to Soviet sources, the aid constituted about 4 percent of Soviet war production, most of it coming in the 1944–45 period, after the battle of Stalingrad, the turning point on the eastern front. In total, it amounted to over $10 billion from the United States and £428 million from Great Britain.

There is sometimes a sense in the West that Allied assistance to Russia during the war is not well remembered or appreciated. The actual Soviet perspective is perhaps best expressed by their response to this assertion, which, in effect, says, "You paid with steel to defeat Nazi Germany, we paid with blood."

Stalin and the "Great Patriotic War" in Soviet Perspective

Overall, the Stalinist era demonstrated the near-total control of the Russian Party leadership over the Russian population and their ability to mobilize that population toward the national objectives of industrialization and national defense. The sacrifices of the Soviet people whether brought on by shared goals or coercion have been monumental in these efforts. From the perspective of the problems that dominate the U.S.-Soviet relationship today, these sacrifices suggest that U.S. measures designed to squeeze Soviet leaders economically to achieve political objectives are probably futile. The Soviet nation, Party and people have simply come through too much at too high a price to surrender to pressures of such a nature.

Just as it is hard to visualize the death and destruction of the detonation from a single nuclear warhead, it is equally hard to visualize the magnitude of the price paid by the Soviet Union in what they call the "Great Patriotic War." The numbers alone defy comprehension: one-tenth of the

Russian population (over 20 million people) killed,[2] close to half of the territory that had been the primary industrial and agricultural region destroyed, first as the German armies moved eastward, and then again as the Russian armies drove them back to the west.

Beyond the death and destruction, there is also the impact the war has had, and continues to have, on the Soviet government and people and their view of the world. Hitler's betrayal of the Russian-German nonaggression pact and German atrocities against the Russian people during the war stay etched in the Russian consciousness. The hesitancy of the British and French to join in a united front to stop German aggression before the war and the allied reticence on the long-promised second front, left the Soviet Union carrying the bulk of the fighting against Germany for almost three years, from 1941–44. Against this background, we can see how the Alliance, loosely tied from the start, collapsed quickly in the early postwar period, as the Red Army remained in Eastern Europe to help establish Communist satellite regimes loyal to Moscow. This was the start of the cold war.

---

[2]This figure is approximately the number of people who would be killed in either the Soviet Union or the United States should the other launch a first strike against that country's long-range missile and bomber forces.

Chapter 4

Measuring the Cold War: From the Iron Curtain to the Cuban Missile Crisis

With the defeat of Germany and Japan, the end of World War II left an enormous power vacuum in both central Europe and east Asia, a power vacuum that, given the impact of the war on Britain and the internal problems of China and France, only the Soviet Union and the United States could fill. As a result, the postwar world rapidly developed into a contest for the "spheres of influence" each would occupy, despite the fact that American leaders, in contrast to both Churchill and Stalin, had since the days of Woodrow Wilson, rejected the idea of "spheres of influence" in favor of self-determination.

Laying Blame for the Cold War

Defying its name, the origin of the cold war is a hotly debated topic among political analysts everywhere, and particularly between the United States and the Soviet Union. The American viewpoint had tended to emphasize the following causes:

1. The historic suspicion and distrust with which Russia has viewed the West since the time of the first tsars;
2. The almost paranoid Soviet desire for security, which manifested itself in the Soviet desire to control bordering nations;
3. Soviet stationing of large conventional land forces on the perimeter of central and southern Europe;

4. Soviet use of the occupation of the countries of Eastern Europe as a first step in reinstituting revolutionary goals of the Comintern;
5. The personality of Stalin, which was seen to embody all of his country's insecurities and imperial ambitions;
6. Soviet failure to undertake a major demobilization at the end of the war;
7. The "domino theory," which suggested that if one single country was lost to the Soviet Union, eventually all would fall like a row of dominoes.

In laying blame for the cold war at the feet of the West, the Soviet viewpoint has tended to emphasize:

1. The threatening presence of U.S. bases on its borders and our continual development, stockpiling and deployment of nuclear weapons and the means to deliver them;
2. The efforts of "U.S. imperialists" to dominate Europe, made most apparent in American reconstruction aid under the Marshall Plan;
3. U.S. efforts to block reparations due the Soviets from Germany and Iran and Soviet desires to improve their security by gaining easier access to the Mediterranean;
4. U.S. interference in Greek elections and the Greek civil war against the interests of indigenous pro-Communist forces;
5. Hysterical and unfounded anti-Communist rhetoric among Western leaders, especially Churchill, Truman and the U.S. Congress.

The Fractured Alliance

From 1943 to 1945, the leaders of the Allied countries met three times: at Tehran (November–December 1943), Yalta (February 1945) and Potsdam (July 1945). The three main subjects of discussion were (1) the treatment of Germany and her allies after the war; (2) territorial alignments and realignments; and (3) formation of the United Nations.

Regarding territorial demands, Soviet desires were largely met. They acquired the Baltic states—Latvia, Lithuania and

Estonia—as well as parts of Germany, Poland and Czecho-slovakia. They also were guaranteed the right to garrison troops in Poland, Hungary and Romania in order to protect their lines of communication into Germany and Austria, both under four-power occupation. Here, as well as in the remaining Eastern European countries under Soviet occupation, the Soviet Union agreed to hold free elections.

But the Red Army, which had driven the Germans out of the Soviet Union across Eastern Europe into Germany, stayed on as occupying forces through the summer of 1945. By mid-August, *less than one week* after the Japanese surrender that ended the hostilities of World War II, the Grand Alliance that had held up for four years of war with Germany and Japan began to unravel. U.S. and British officials questioned the legitimacy of the provisional governments that had been set up in Bulgaria, Romania, Hungary and Poland, charging, in the words of British Foreign Secretary Bevin, "One kind of totalitarianism is being replaced by another."

The Soviet press responded to these attacks with challenges to the Allied supervision of Greek elections. The cold war was on.

On March 5, 1946, Churchill, now out of power but still a towering political figure in Great Britain and the U.S., delivered a now-famous speech at Fulton, Missouri. Long a staunch anti-Communist, Churchill urged a continued military and political alliance between the two English-speaking countries against the Soviet Union:

From Stettin [Poland] in the Baltic to Trieste [Yugoslavia] in the Adriatic, an *iron curtain* has descended across the Continent. All these famous cities and the populations around them lie in the Soviet sphere and are subject, in one form or another, not only to Soviet influence but to a very high and increasing measure of control from Moscow . . .

Soviet reaction to the Churchill speech was visceral. *Pravda* condemned the speech immediately as "poisonous" and a week later Stalin called Churchill a "war-monger" comparable to Hitler.

At the outset, American opinion on relations with the Soviet Union was divided. Former Vice President Henry

Wallace, now Secretary of Commerce, was urging we destroy our atomic arsenal immediately, arguing, "the real peace we need now is between the U.S. and Russia." At the same time, the national commander of the American Legion was claiming, "We ought to aim an atomic bomb right now at Moscow—and save one for Tito, too!" As an omen of things to come, under pressure from Secretary of State Byrnes, in September 1946 President Truman was forced to ask for Wallace's resignation from the Cabinet.

The first direct issue of conflict occurred over the Allied departure from Iran, scheduled for March 2, 1946. Great Britain and the Soviet Union had moved troops into Iran in 1942 to keep the Axis powers out. At Tehran in 1943, they agreed to withdraw six months after the war ended. By September, it appeared to the British that the Soviets were going to annex Azerbaijan, a province of Iran.

When Stalin indicated his intention was to prolong the occupation in order to be assured of a Soviet share in Iranian oil as part of its war reparations, Britain and the U.S. appealed to the United Nations for intervention. When the issue was resolved on the basis of a promise that the oil would be delivered (a promise later repudiated by the Iranian Parliament), Iran became in effect an Anglo-American protectorate, the first move in what the Soviets saw as a grand conspiracy to encircle their country.

A major factor underlying the actions of the British and American governments in Iran was the messianic zeal of the Soviet Communist Party in its support for the efforts of the Communist parties of France and Italy to gain control of those weakened postwar governments. The efforts convinced the Western powers that Soviet imperialism and proletarian revolution were once again motivating Moscow.

In succeeding months, the conflict shifted to the eastern Mediterranean where American and British intervention were able to stem Soviet support for indigenous Communist rebels in their efforts to achieve control of Greece. Soviet efforts to secure ports in the Dardanelles from Turkey in order to gain access to the Mediterranean through the narrow Straits and retrocession to Russia of parts of Turkey also ran into British and American roadblocks.

Against strong opposition, particularly from isolationist Republicans in the Congress, Truman asked Congress for $400 million in aid for Greece and Turkey. In a speech that conjured up the evils of Communism and the "Red Menace" in the harshest terms, Truman enunciated his famous "Truman Doctrine": " . . . totalitarian regimes, imposed on free peoples by direct or indirect aggression, undermine the foundations of international peace and hence the security of the U.S. . . . " (Contrary to the impression given to the American public by President Truman, neither country at the time was a democracy, Greece being ruled by a Fascist monarchy and Turkey by a one-party dictatorship.)

The rhetoric of the Truman Doctrine and the policy of "containment" that followed prepared the American public for the Marshall Plan for the reconstruction of Europe inaugurated in late 1947. Over the next four years, the U.S. government spent $20 billion on the Marshall Plan as well as billions more for military and economic aid under the "Mutual Security Program."

Back in the USSR

Even as the war ended, Stalin had begun reestablishing the relative isolation from the West that had been the hallmark of the previous seven centuries of Russian history. To begin, Soviet troops and prisoners of war returning from central Europe were "reeducated" to the Soviet way of life before they were permitted to reenter Soviet society. This included considerable political indoctrination, and for many who had been German POWs, including Alexander Solzhenitsyn, internment in labor camps in Siberia.

This turn inward was also taking place on the economic, social and cultural levels. Economic ties with the West were gradually removed. Soviet science was given a special status and distinguished from Western "bourgeois" science. Emphasis was placed on the great Russian people, language and culture at the expense of minority nationalities, which were drawn closer in under Moscow's wing.

Accompanying this process was the gradual reestablishment of the Communist Party as the supreme authority and symbol of Soviet unity in the country. The wartime elevation of religion, Russian nationalism and military heroes such as Marshal Zhukov was reversed, and the Party itself was purged of those individuals who had joined during the war and did not have the aptitude and commitment for the Party's political role in the country.

In September of 1947, the Communist Information Bureau (Cominform), to some extent the successor to the defunct Comintern, was created to coordinate international Communist activities in Europe and elsewhere. Its opening manifesto declared:

> Two opposite political lines have formed: on the one side is the policy of the USSR and democratic countries directed toward undermining imperialism and strengthening democracy, on the other side is the policy of the USA and England directed toward strengthening imperialism and strangling democracy.

This concept of the world divided into two opposing camps would be a fixation for Stalin and his successors for the next two decades.

Hot Spots in a Cold War

The Cold War was not without its flashes of open confrontation. The first occurred in Berlin, the former capital of Nazi Germany. In March 1948, the joint Allied administration of the city collapsed, and two months later the Soviet government cut off all land and water transportation between the Western Zone and West Berlin, isolated well inside the Russian Zone in the heart of what is now East Germany. The possible use of military force to reach Berlin was considered—General Lucius Clay proposed opening the highways with tanks—but after a month a decision was made to airlift food and supplies to the beleaguered city and eventually the Soviet blockade was lifted. As a direct response to the Soviet action, a year later the Western allies oversaw the organization of the German Federal Republic (West Germany) in the combined British, French and American Zones. Within a few months, the Soviet Union responded by creating the German Democratic Republic (East Germany).

In this same period, there were other important developments in East-West tensions, described in more detail later in this book, including (1) the victory of Mao's Communists in China (1949); (2) the founding of NATO (1949); the explosion of the first Soviet atomic device (1949); and (4) the

Truman decision to begin hydrogen bomb development (1950).

In June 1950, the global "Cold War" became a localized "hot war" with the invasion of South Korea by Communist North Korea with the avowed purpose of reunifying the country divided at the end of World War II. Frustrated with the recent loss of China to the Communists and the tensions of the Cold War, the United States rushed to the defense of South Korea with claims of Soviet inspiration behind the attack and demands that monolithic Communism be stopped. After three years, the intervention of the Red Chinese Army and the loss of 54,000 American lives, the fighting ended with the border between the two countries essentially where it had been at the outset.

Purging the Soviet Conscience: Khrushchev and De-Stalinization

On March 5, 1953, Joseph Stalin succumbed to a fatal stroke. Dressed in full military uniform, he was laid to rest in public view alongside Lenin in the massive marble tomb in Red Square. After two years of collective leadership that included Georgi Malenkov, Stalin's heir apparent, Nikita Khrushchev, formerly head of the Communist Party in Moscow and the Ukraine and a Party activist since before the Revolution, emerged as sole Party Leader. In 1958 he assumed full control of the country, as head of both Party and government.

By summer of the year following Stalin's death, reverence for the departed leader or *vodhz,* as he was known, began to fade. However, the gradual deflation of Stalin's public image was barely a hint of the outright denouncement of Stalin that was to come at the Twentieth Congress of the Soviet Communist Party in 1956. Khrushchev gave a lengthy, vitriolic speech accusing Stalin of a laundry list of crimes against the Soviet people, state and the Communist movement, ranging from "deviating from Leninism" to interfering with military operations and practicing "brutal violence" and "torture." It was a massive indictment, but one that was given in secret to the 1,436 Congress delegates and is yet to be published in the Soviet Union. Later in the Khrushchev era, Stalin's image was revived somewhat and even further restored under Brezhnev, but his stature still remains far below that of Lenin in Soviet history.

Missiles and Missile Gaps in the Khrushchev Era

During his period as head of the Soviet Union, Khrushchev had to confront major economic problems, especially in the agricultural sector (see Chapter 7), and acknowledge the substantial lag between Soviet military capabilities and those of the United States and its allies, especially in the number of nuclear weapons and delivery systems. In the area of missiles and space development, Soviet achievements were dramatic. In August 1957, the Soviet Union launched the first intercontinental ballistic missile (ICBM) and on October 4, 1957, shocked the world by launching the first man-made satellite, *Sputnik,* into orbit. Two years later, a Soviet satellite had photographed the dark side of the moon, and after numerous other test launches, in April 1961, the Soviet Union launched the first man, Yuri Gargarin, into space (and two years later, the first woman, Valentina Tereshkova).

Soviet space achievements were a major propaganda coup for the Soviet Union, one they exploited to the fullest with attributions of their success to the virtues of Leninism, socialism and the Soviet people. But in the late 1950s, Soviet successes in space spurred Khrushchev to use the associated threat that the Soviet Union would soon have a significant edge in ICBMs—an ICBM "missile gap," as John Kennedy would describe it in the 1960 presidential campaign. He tried to use this advantage to extract foreign relations concessions, most notably in Berlin, where in the summer of 1961 he attempted without success to dislodge the Western powers.

By the fall of 1961 the ICBM missile gap myth was exploded by newly operating U.S. spy satellites. In fact, it had become clear that by the mid-1960s there would likely be an ICBM missile gap substantially in the favor of the U.S. (The Soviet Union had more medium and intermediate range ballistic missiles—MRBMs and IRBMs—than the U.S., but they could not reach the U.S. from Soviet territory.) In addition, the U.S. had a substantial advantage in its bomber fleet, which could reliably penetrate existing Soviet defenses.

Khrushchev was frustrated with his failure to have gained only propaganda advantages from his missile and space successes and the accompanying loss of prestige at home and in the Communist world for both his foreign and domestic policies. As a consequence, in the spring of 1962 he decided to try to offset the upcoming American advantage in ICBMs by placing MRBMs and IRBMs in Cuba, thereby increasing by 50 percent the number of Soviet missiles that could reach the U.S. When a resolute President Kennedy demanded removal of the missiles or face having the missiles destroyed by U.S. air strikes, Khrushchev chose the former course.

The failure in Berlin, the exposure of the mythical missile gap and the aborted Cuban missile effort led the Soviet Union to once again seek rapprochement with the United States on arms control and to try to establish some basis for détente. But by then Cuba and other failures were helping to bring about the demise of Khrushchev as leader of the Soviet Union.

In October 1964, Khrushchev was toppled from power by a coup organized by a clique of his closest associates. Ironically, the charges against him were in part strongly reminiscent of those that he had leveled against Stalin in his famous denunciation of the former leader in 1956—creating a "personality cult," violating norms of "collective leadership," "rule by fiat" and causing disorganization in Soviet industry and agriculture. But the charges also included such behavior as "bragging and blustering" and "harebrained scheming" more unique to the rotund, loquacious dictator.

The ouster of Khrushchev brought to power two of his longtime protégés—Leonid Brezhnev as First Secretary of the Party and Alexei Kosygin as Chairman of the USSR Council of Ministers. Nikolai Podgorny became President of the USSR. From his position as Party Secretary, Brezhnev gradually emerged by the late 1960s as the senior partner in the triumverate, remaining the dominant leader in the country until his death in 1982.

Did the Cold War Ever Thaw?

In 1964, the legacy that Brezhnev inherited from Stalin, Lenin and Khrushchev before him included a massive military capability, although still second to the United States; an authoritarian political system with the Party unchallenged at the top; a long-sought buffer of satellite states on the Soviet western border; and an as yet unfulfilled promise of the triumph of socialism over capitalism in terms of the quality of life for Soviet citizens. While the cold war had eased as each side pulled back from the Cuban confrontation, the Western capitalist democracies appeared resolute in their determination to meet Soviet challenges on a global scale.

The cold war occurred at a time when in Western eyes the Soviet bear put his worst paw forward. Political freedom, a touchstone of Western war efforts, was brutally suppressed with the Soviet expansion into Eastern Europe. The volume of hostile rhetoric from Moscow was turned to full pitch, playing to the worst fears of the U.S. public and Congress. In turn, Western actions in central Europe and the Mediterranean were perceived by the Soviet Union, rightly or wrongly, as threats to their security. These actions played in to the historic Russian suspicion and distrust of the West which had been reinvigorated by the trouble-plagued World War II Alliance.

PART II
Life Outside the Kremlin: Soviet Economy, Society and Culture

Chapter 5

Rough and Smooth Spots on the Soviet Bear: Soviet National Character and Culture

Who are these people who sit with their individual and collective fingers on the proverbial "button" that would launch nuclear missiles, initiating nuclear war and our certain destruction? What are they like? What is it in their character and culture that keeps them building those weapons? What would it take for them to freeze that effort and reverse the arms race? And why haven't they pushed the button before now? After all they've done, can we really trust them? Can we even communicate with them any better than we might, say, with a real Siberian brown bear? And how do *they* feel about *us?*

This chapter asserts that the answers to these questions are well removed from the "front lines" of the U.S.-Soviet conflict. Rather, they lie in an understanding of the common threads of a people who produced and tolerated one of the most despotic, totalitarian states in history, yet also produced some of the world's richest literature on the human condition, a society that manufactures massive SS-18 missiles but also embraces the subtleties of ballet and chess as representative forms of its high and low culture.

If we are going to deal with the Soviet Union we *must* develop the means of understanding the character and personality of the Soviet nation and people. This understanding is essential if we are to communicate with them in a language and terms we both understand, since the consequences of misunderstanding could be as small as a minor insult, or as large as a nuclear war.

The history of Russia and the Soviet Union in Part I showed us how the long-standing desire for authoritarian social and political structures, a paranoid concern with security and a simultaneous admiration and distrust for Western society are essential themes in Russian culture. We will find these themes recurring again and again in subsequent discussions of the Soviet political system, Soviet foreign and military policy and attitudes toward nuclear war and explorations of future prospects for the Soviet Union and U.S.-Soviet relations.

The Physical Environment

It is sometimes said that Russians resemble Americans. Indeed, despite some rather hefty differences in history and ideology, there are similarities between the two countries. Foremost among these similarities is the fact that both nationalities have been shaped by the struggle for survival on vast continental land masses in a hard and hostile climate, although the land mass is greater and the climate much more severe in the USSR.

In our somewhat comparable expanses of land, we share with the Soviet Union a similar frontier heritage and the advantages of access to extensive natural resources as well as the disadvantages that vast territories pose for transportation, communications and political control. And perhaps just as important as the tangible advantages and disadvantages of a large, resource-laden territory are the mind-sets nurtured by such vastness. The Soviet peoples and the Americans share a preference for spaciousness and adventure.

The harsh climate in many regions of the Soviet Union has had an effect on the people's outlook. Gray skies characterize much of the country much of the year. Cold winters in the northern regions put severe constraints on human activity in the towns and villages. Rampant alcoholism among the Soviets is also sometimes attributed to the harsh climate.

The Soviet land mass carries with it one characteristic we in America have not had to confront—the absence of defensible geographical frontiers separating the country from external enemies. As Chapter 1 suggested, Russia was never a very secure place to live, and Russian leaders and peoples have been obsessively concerned about defense throughout history. Together with the many centuries of isolation from a more advanced European society to the West, this insecurity has created in the Russian and Soviet people a fear and distrust of foreigners. As the Soviet Union has achieved the status of a global power and its elites have increased their contact with the outside world, these xenophobic attitudes could well be changing, but they remain deeply rooted in the population at large.

On a more positive side, the Russians are strongly devoted to their land, creating in them a patriotism that is stronger and deeper than ours. Medieval Russian chronicles made much of the symbol of the Russian land, and nineteenth-century literature and landscape painting reinforced it. It remains in the Soviet era a very potent idea and symbol of national identity.

History: The Not So "New Soviet Man"

It is an article of faith of the Communist Party of the Soviet Union that on November 7, 1917, the Revolution gave birth to a "new Soviet man." In ideological terms, this man, unlike his forebears, would be cooperative rather than competitive; communal rather than individualistic; altruistic rather than self-interested.

Long-standing modes of Russian thought and behavior under the tsars could not be wiped out overnight, however. Centuries of conditioning in tyranny and despotism, first under the Mongols and later, during six centuries of tsarist rule, nurtured a don't-rock-the-boat attitude among the Russian (now Soviet) citizenry. To question the authority of the state often resulted in various punishments ranging from loss of privileges to loss of life. Communal life in the peasant villages reinforced obedience to authority. Decision-making placed a high value on consensus, on what might be called the "group yes." Everyone must agree; those who don't can leave the village. Thus, it was better to keep silent than to invoke the certain wrath of the authorities. In fact, having lived so long in a condition of subservience to higher authority, many Russians equate freedom with anarchy.

When in the nineteenth century Russia attempted to catch up with the economic developments in the West, that effort was undertaken without the establishment of a comparable political culture, emphasizing freedom and individual initiative. As a result, there was considerable intellectual debate about the place and content of Russian culture. "Are we part of the West or does Russian spiritual culture have roots of its own that are different from those of the West, e.g., Orthodox vs. Catholic religious roots?" In contrast to the U.S., where we accept our having major roots in European culture, this question has occupied Russian thinkers from the enforced modernization of Peter the Great onward, producing a "Western-Slavophile" schism that continues to the present day. Not just in Soviet politics, but also in literature, art and philosophy, there is a cosmopolitan, international, and pro-Western outlook set against an isolationist, Slavophile, anti-Western, anti-détente outlook.

Following the Revolution, the ideal of the "new Soviet man" still placed the individual subordinate to the state. In addition, the methods for producing such a citizen were analogous to the means that the tsars had employed in subjugating the population to their ends centuries earlier: a system of controlled privilege and coercive power, built upon a strong central government, a massive bureaucracy and a secret police, which, together with the inviolable physical characteristics of the geography, insured a distinctly "Russian" character to Soviet society. Further, instead of a tsarist aristocracy that justified its power by claiming the "divine right of kings," the Soviet Union was governed from the outset by a charismatic leader and a minority political organization that justified its right to rule by means of a new "theology," that of Marxism-Leninism. Marxism-Leninism had overtones of more than just a secular religion; it also embodied the deification of science, with accompanying frequent references to scientific socialism. All of the elements were marshalled in a massive collective effort to transform a predominantly agrarian society into a technologically advanced industrial state, creating a system that came to be characterized as "totalitarianism."

While much that is old, deep-rooted and characteristically Russian survives under the mask of the "new Soviet man," one should not underestimate the novelty of the concept and the changes it has caused in typical Soviet behavior. The average Soviet citizen, especially in urban areas, is in many ways *not* like his forebears in tsarist times. He has a degree of punctuality and accuracy and labor discipline and a sense of technical and machine values largely unknown before the Revolution, even if still inferior to much of the West. He has absorbed much of the materialistic, anti-religious, scientific-empirical and production-oriented outlook of Marxist-Leninist ideology. These features, together with dynamism, Party spirit and discipline have from the very outset been more central to the ideal of the "new Soviet man" than the ideological tenets of cooperation, communalism (long a Russian peasant ideal) and altruism.

Soviet Culture High and Low

The essential character of the Soviet citizen and his Russian forebears is manifest in both the "low" (popular) and "high" culture of their societies. The development of this culture, like the development of the Russian and Soviet national character, for a time took place at a distance from the European culture to the West. However, when Russian high culture blossomed in the nineteenth and early twentieth centuries, it was profoundly influenced by traditional European forms and ideas, despite its native folklore themes.

The Soviet Union is heir to an extraordinary cultural tradition rooted in a rich diversity of folk and ethnic influences, an unquenchable intelligentsia and an historic search for spiritual solace in art. All have contributed to Russian creative achievements. Moreover, the limits that the state has imposed on artistic expression since the Revolution have often served only to make genuine art more highly valued because it is so hard to come by. In this officially atheistic, utilitarian and collective society, the vacuum that is filled by religion, open political discourse, privacy or the creature comforts in Western society is often filled by books, poetry, music and other art forms, which offer an intellectual and spiritual release from ordinary life. In the words of Soviet poet Andrei Voznesensky:

> We have no philosophers or political commentators in your [American] sense, no folk singers with moral messages, and no religion for most people. So there is a vacuum. People need something for their spirit, and they turn to poets. Some come for entertainment and others for religion or politics or philosophy. They expect all this from the poet. That's why he is so important in Russia. (Hedrick Smith, *The Russians,* p. 508)

For the Soviet citizen, the role of culture is perhaps of even more importance than for a Westerner. The tensions of collective life in a highly politicized society create the potential for conflict between public and private existence—between the outer life of the person as a member of a mass society and his private, inner life as an individual. It is one of the ironies of Soviet life that in this most politicized of societies, and despite conscious Party efforts to blend public and private life, little or no leisure time and conversation are occupied with political concerns and discourse beyond that perfunctorily required by the state and Party; public and private remain separate realms.

A Nation of Bookworms

The Soviet Union is a nation of readers. It has been said the Soviet society is literate the way ours is obsessed with television. Foreign visitors report the frequency with which people in public places such as parks and subways can be found reading everything from *Pravda* to pamphlets on foreign policy to novels. The great Russian novels of the past and Russian literature generally are of critical importance to the Soviet citizen, and the Russians have a rich literary inventory from which to choose.

As late as the late seventeenth century, Russian literature consisted mostly of sermons, saints' lives and ballads of heroic exploits, mostly written in an archaic Church Slavonic language, the literary achievements of the European Renaissance and its themes of freedom and individualism having had no counterpart in Russia. However, under Peter the Great, Russia opened its doors to the West, and by the end of the eighteenth century its upper classes were familiar with contemporary German, French and English literature.

The Golden Age of Russian literature began with a great poet named Aleksandr Sergeyevich Pushkin (1799-1837), who did for Russian what Shakespeare did for English and Goethe did for German. In the endless variety of his themes and his treatment of them, both in prose and poetry, Pushkin projected enormous compassion with all forms of human suffering and a readiness to "co-suffer" with these victims. In such works as *Eugene Onegin,* Pushkin portrays characters who are neither heroes nor villains, but most often victims of fate, open to the experiences of life but skeptical as to its overall meaning.

Pushkin was followed by Nikolai Gogol, whose tale of Chichikov, with his get-rich-quick scheme of selling the title deeds for dead serfs to wealthy landowners (*Dead Souls*, 1842), introduces the reader to an entire array of Russian social types that parade through successive Russian novels; Mikhail Lermontov (*Hero of Our Time*, 1840), whose early works were severely censored; and Ivan Turgenev (*Fathers and Sons*, 1862), the first Russian novelist to be read and admired in the West.

Two names can sum up the culminating achievements of the nineteenth-century Russian novel: Leo Tolstoy and Fyodor Dostoyevsky. Tolstoy is well-known for one of the greatest novels in the history of literature, *War and Peace* (1869). In vividly portraying characters against the impersonal backdrop of historical events such as the Napoleon wars, Tolstoy paves the way for such twentieth-century novels as Boris Pasternak's *Dr. Zhivago* and Mikhail Sholokov's *And Quiet Flows the Don,* both set in the Russian Revolution and Civil War. *Anna Karenina*, Tolstoy's story of a woman who defies societal convention in the name of love, is one of the finest examples of the sympathetic treatment of human suffering for which Russian literature is renowned. Dostoyevsky is best known for his psychological novels, including such masterpieces as *Crime and Punishment, The Idiot* and *The Brothers Karamazov*. In *The Possessed,* he anticipated the Russian Revolution of 1917 almost fifty years before it happened, predicting that revolution in his country would start "from unlimited freedom" and "arrive at unlimited despotism."

To read any of these novels, often as ambitious in length as in content, is to open a window onto the Russian mind. They explore many of the most elemental questions of human existence as well as the universal sufferings and moral dilemmas of all men. Russians say a great writer is like a "second government"—a moral authority. Modern-day Soviet citizens read these Russian classics in their leisure, and bookstores and libraries are hard-pressed to keep them on the shelves. They are also read in the schools, where whole armies of Soviet teachers are inclined toward interpretations of their themes that point toward the Russian Revolution.

Russian music has also made a tremendous contribution to the civilization of the West, providing such geniuses as Tchaikovsky, Moussorgsky, Prokofiev, Rimsky-Korsakov, Rachmaninoff, Stravinsky and many others. The world of dance has also benefitted from its great Russian contributors; present-day audiences are delighted by such stars as Barishnikov and Nureyev.

Socialist Realism: Man Loves Tractor

During the 1920s, there was a demand for politically committed art, but it was an open-ended situation that allowed for experimentation and pluralism. But in the Stalinist era, art, like everything else, came under the control of the state. In 1934, "socialist realism" became the standard for artistic expression and substantial censorship was imposed. Russian writers in the nineteenth century had to write under the restrictions of censorship as well, but the censors were not very sophisticated and they were able to write *mezhdu strok,* "between the lines and on the margins," thus conveying their intended message. This new Soviet art was to be patriotic in theme, comprehensible and inspiring to the masses. As a tool of the Party and state, art became a vehicle for propaganda and was obliged to portray life not as it is, with all its imperfections, but rather as it should be and ultimately would be in the perfect socialist society.

Not surprisingly, this purposeful, political standard took a heavy toll on artistic expression for a long time, for art, more than any other form of expression, depends upon innovation and freedom of choice. For artists in the Soviet Union, experimentalism became suspect, abstraction taboo. That art officially sanctioned by the Stalinist regime more often than not proved mediocre and unimaginative. For example, in literature, socialist realism meant a preponderance of what some have termed the man-loves-tractor theme, in which inspirational stories of devoted workers glorify the achievements of the workers' state.

With the death of Stalin in 1953, the all-pervasive totalitarian control of the arts under his regime gave way to alternating currents of partial relaxation of controls and reimposed repression under both Khrushchev and Brezhnev. In the early post-Stalinist period, the leading edge of artistic dissent was in the literary journal *Novyi Mir* (New World), whose pages contained attacks on the effort of the Party to limit what was acceptable in art to the standards of "socialist realism."

Following the lead of *Novyi Mir*, a number of well-known books came out in the period that had decidedly anti-Stalinist themes, among the best known of which is Alexander Solzhenitsyn's *One Day in the Life of Ivan Denisovich*, depicting life in one of Stalin's labor camps. Boris Pasternak's *Dr. Zhivago* was also published in this period, but not in the Soviet Union (nor has it been since). There was a backlash in Party circles against this new literature and other modern art forms and the remaining years of the Khrushchev era and most of the Brezhnev era saw continuous conflict between the regime and writers and other artists.

While the opportunities for creative artistic expression in the Soviet Union are constrained, by no means is all Soviet art and literature propaganda. There are new currents in what is approved for publication and in the underground artistic and intellectual ferment among the intelligentsia.

Ironically, the greater the effort by the state to limit the scope of unauthorized art, the more highly valued such art becomes. Soviet citizens value highly their access to cultural events and classical Russian and foreign literature. Its political features aside, the Soviet Union in the 1980s is an organic, creative society, and although substantial censorship exists, political controls and censorship are by no means those of the Stalinist era and are, in fact, often erratic and ineffective. Thus everything in art and literature is not black and white, official and unofficial. While some important and well-known Soviet artists and writers now live outside the country—Solzhenitsyn, the poet Joseph Brodsky, the ballet dancer Mikhail Baryshnikov—there is good new writing, plays, art and movies dealing with such themes as the lot of the peasants under collectivization (thereby asking some profound questions about the meaning of the Revolution), the importance of individual values, and Russian spirit and tradition (where there is a substantial Slavophile trend).

Popular Culture

Artistic expression and "high" culture aside, what can be said about "low," or "popular," culture in the Soviet Union? What do Soviet citizens do in their free time? Where, for example, do Party elites go on their vacations? What does a factory worker do for leisure? How do university students spend their weekends? And forgetting about Tchaikovsky for a minute—is there such a thing as Russian rock 'n' roll?

Official Soviet government accounts of how Soviet citizens spend their leisure time focus on glowing reports of organized sports teams, union-subsidized vacation passes and youth camps and outings sponsored by Komsomol, the youth branch of the Communist Party. Unfortunately, a shortage of official facilities and programs means that the majority of citizens must fend for themselves on their days and nights off, but Soviet citizens are no less ingenious than Americans about entertaining themselves. They devote their leisure time to impromptu and inexpensive diversions: for men, there are chess and dominoes—enhanced by a good deal of betting—in the city parks; for the young there is always open-air hiking and camping in the summer and ice skating and hockey in the winter, and, of course, chess year-round. In the fall, the national craze for mushroom hunting brings virtually everyone out into the much-loved Russian countryside, as does cross-country skiing in the winter.

Television in the Soviet Union is widely available—there is now one television set for every five citizens. Television continues to expand into the rural areas, but the programs are not of particularly high quality (in this respect, the U.S. and Soviet Union probably have parity). Programming carries a cross section of travelogues, talk shows, speeches by Party officials, sports events, concerts, films, children's programming and popular entertainment shows. In addition, an irritating amount of propaganda—as irritating, no doubt, as American commercials—is broadcast between television shows and in movie theaters, another popular Soviet diversion.

In subject matter, "the Great Patriotic War" (World War II) is as popular in the Soviet Union as Westerns used to be in the U.S., and stories of Soviet master spies in Nazi Germany are quite common. Script writers are required to fill a quota of movies covering the lives of Lenin and other leading historical figures, and movies glorifying exceptionally dedicated workers in remarkably efficient factories are widely distributed. But there are many Soviet movie productions of exceptional quality, especially films of classical novels—*The Idiot, War and Peace, Crime and Punishment*, etc.—which drew wide international acclaim. Some recent popular films such as *Moscow Does Not Believe in Tears* explore new themes, such as the search for personal spiritual values, as well as some of the classical themes touched on by the nineteenth-century masters.

In the Soviet Union, as in the United States, sports are enormously popular. The Soviet Union fields excellent soccer, ice hockey, basketball and gymnastics teams and in recent years has consistently won more Olympic medals than any other country. Sports programming draws the broadest viewership of all television shows, and the attraction of sports is to strong that the Russian word for "fan," *bolel'shchik*, literally translates as "one who has become ill."

Contemporary pop music has a great appeal for young people all over the world, and young Soviet citizens are no exception. Some of what goes on in the "new music" scene is, of necessity, small scale and underground, since radical departures from traditional music forms are officially taboo. However, many "rock gruppas" have been permitted to perform publicly and have drawn a national audience among Soviet youth, although the general consensus is that popular musicians are permitted to do a fraction of their own music in performance as long as the major proportion is pro-Soviet in theme. The fine line performers and artists must generally walk was amply demonstrated by the recent experience of one of the best-known rock groups, called "Time Machine." After being chosen as the most popular group of 1981 by readers of *Komsomolskaya Pravda,* the official daily of the Young Communist League, the group was subsequently denounced in the same paper as "un-Russian," raucous and loaded with "dangerous ideas."

Convergence or Divergence in the Russian National Character and Culture

The recent experience of "Time Machine" highlights the unresolved conflict in the Soviet Union between Slavophile/isolationist sentiments and the conflicting Westernizing/international impulse, which goes well beyond matters of character and culture and hangs heavily as well on Soviet divisions vis-à-vis the U.S. on nuclear weapons issues. Just as we speak of a "Fortress America" sentiment in our country, a comparable and more extreme sentiment prevails in the Soviet Union. "The West cannot be trusted. The West is corrupt. The only way to deal with them is through building defenses and holding them at arm's length. Only in this way can superior Slavic roots and culture be preserved." But as in the U.S. before the two World Wars, this isolationism is also rebuked as naive and short-sighted. "The West cannot be assumed away. The world is just too small and the West too powerful to hope to escape either. There is room for the Soviet Union to learn from the West and expand Soviet global status while still maintaining the essential character of Russian society." These are the two unresolved sentiments—divergence or convergence—that the Soviet people and leaders bring to the U.S.-Soviet relationship and to the dilemma of nuclear war.

Chapter 6

From Cradle to Grave in the USSR: Probing the Everyday Life of the Soviet Citizen

Many Americans assume that if we could just circumvent the Soviet Communist Party and government and get to the "real people" in that country, we would find that they're "just folks," and the enmity between our two countries would disappear like ice and snow in a spring thaw. Given the well-recognized barriers to this occurrence in the prevailing environment, it still remains essential to ask whether or not the candle is worth the flame, whether in fact the common denominators of human existence—birth, life, childhood, adolescence, maturity, marriage, parenthood, divorce, old age—experienced by real people persist in the Soviet Union next to, and in many ways in spite of, Marxism-Leninism, the omnipresent Party and state, SS-18 missiles and the many deprivations brought on by wars, collectivization, purges and the arms buildup.

It may come as a surprise to many Americans that despite our dramatically different historical traditions and experiences, contemporary political and economic systems and ideologies, a considerable commonality in life experiences—a commonality that does contain the potential for establishing positive relations between our two peoples and countries—does exist for U.S. and Soviet citizens. Yet the special set of circumstances of the Soviet present and past has also given the life of Soviet citizens a particular coloration and cast. "Soviet Life," as the country's English language export magazine is called, *is* different in many ways from that into which the proverbial "average American" is born, reared, works, retires and dies. It is important to comprehend the extent of those differences. First we need to see whether they are important in any larger political sense, and then, in a much more mundane sense, we need to get a "feel" for those people whose government has developed the capability to destroy our very existence.

Children and Childhood

"Our children are our future," Russians are fond of saying, and it is obvious that much time and energy are devoted to insuring a future generation that is healthier and happier than all who have gone before. As a result Russian children are raised with a generous dose of both affection and discipline, both of which are typically more openly demonstrated by the Russians than by their American counterparts. It is not at all uncommon for a complete stranger to be unreservedly affectionate toward a child he sees on a crowded bus or subway; nor is it unusual for that same stranger to rebuke either the child or its parents for any perceived unruly behavior.

It is perhaps ironic that in this society that so prizes its children, the birth rates, especially in the European Soviet Union, including the Russian population, have declined drastically. Limits imposed by crowded housing and women's careers mean that many women, especially in the cities, choose either to have fewer children or no children at all. Perhaps the added care and attention parents and grandparents lavish on their offspring is intensified by the fact that the first child is often also the last.

Despite exaggerated reports in the West of universal communal early childhood care in state-run institutions (only half of Soviet children actually have access to child care outside the home), it is unquestionably the family that has the greatest influence in nurturing the society's future citizens. In fact, the family is the Soviet child's first experience with life in a "collective," since the extended family still exists in the Soviet Union, and almost one-quarter of all apartments are still communal, with kitchens and bath facilities shared by several families. Close family ties continue much longer than in the U.S., in part because the housing shortage in most cities forces many young people to continue to live with their parents until they have children of their own, and sometimes longer. It is not entirely a result of housing shortages that family ties remain strong; indeed, parents in the Soviet Union are often more cognizant of what goes on in their children's lives than are Western parents. In comparison with American society, where age segregation is widespread, in the Soviet Union the worlds of the parents and children overlap a great deal.

Adolescence

In a familiar refrain of parents worldwide, Soviet parents believe that young people have a comfortable existence and take it all too much for granted. American parents who grew up during the 1930s and 1940s and who work hard to keep their teenagers in designer jeans and record albums can easily empathize with their Soviet counterparts, who feel the same way, having suffered the deprivations of World War II and other periods. Soviet parents make substantial personal sacrifices so that their teenage sons and daughters do not have to hold down part-time jobs. At the same time, they provide their children with access to various teenage status symbols, many of which bear striking resemblances to those found in the West.

Soviet young people are especially fond of Western contemporary music and most fashionable clothing among the youth is quite likely to be made out of denim. Nonetheless, these hallmarks of young people worldwide have a different significance for Soviet youth than for Americans. Western music and popular culture, originally symbolic of American youth's rejection of parental affluence and values, have become highly prized—and priced—commodities for Soviet youth, who consider them a mark of status and the good life and a link to youth culture worldwide. Perhaps more in keeping with the materialism and seeming political indifference of the American 1950s, Soviet young people are eager to acquire at least the outer accoutrements of their capitalist counterparts.

Not surprisingly, Party officials share the concern of parents over the nonchalance of this indulged, materialistic younger generation with its lack of idealism and ideological conviction. However, it is not open rebellion but a quiet cynicism that characterizes Soviet youth sixty years after the Revolution. Adolescence is an age for reflection and reevaluation in any culture, and Soviet young people are by no means immune. Some have found a new solace in religion; others in poetry or music.

The popular music group "Time Machine" has even dared to voice some of the doubts of the generation. "I do not believe in promises," the group sings, "and will not do so in the future. There is no point in believing in promises any longer." In a society that allows only optimism and affirmation of the status quo, such skepticism, bordering on pessimism, is suspect and sometimes publicly criticized by the Party. Nonetheless, as noted in Chapter 5, Soviet officials have attempted to moderate rather than entirely abolish these voices among the younger generation. In addition, by a combination of rewarding conformity, creating the anticipation that nonconformity will be punished and then, if it occurs, quashing dissent just as it does in the adult world, the Party believes that ultimately it will be more successful in maintaining its authority.

Soviet Education: Who's Ahead in the Classroom?

Ever since *Sputnik,* there has been a considerable public awareness in the U.S. that we are engaged in a competition with the Soviet Union to see which of us is more adept at educating our young people. In some ways, the battle of the classrooms is just an extension of the arms-race competition because technical, and therefore defense, capabilities depend in some measure on the number of skilled scientists, engineers and technicians in a society. Comparisons between educational systems thus begin to sound like comparisons of the countries' respective nuclear arsenals: Ivan has 1,400 ICBMs, five years of physics, 140 bombers, and eleven years of math; Johnny, on the other hand, can claim only 1,052 ICBMs, only one year of high school chemistry, 348 bombers, but only eight years of math, and grim therefore are the long-term prospects for the American way of life vis-à-vis Soviet Communism, so the argument goes.

Education generally and science education in particular in the U.S. received a tremendous shot in the arm from the federal government after the surprise of *Sputnik* in 1957. From that year to the present, we have frequently heard comparisons between Soviet and American systems of education—and often the argument that the typical American high school curriculum was inadequate next to the rigors of the Soviet system. But it is important to look further than the glowing official reports about education in that country to have an accurate picture of Soviet schools. The Soviet Union has indeed come a long way in public education. Nonetheless, it is evident that there is still a lot of ground to be covered, and though American schools might indeed benefit from a few well-placed reforms, there is no point in being all up in arms about the Soviets being so far ahead in the classroom.

The Soviet Union is prouder of its educational advances than almost any other achievement since the Revolution. The transformation of a largely illiterate peasant society into a modern industrial nation with nearly universal literacy could not have occurred without significant advances in the educational system. Education (including intensive political indoctrination at all levels) is viewed by the state as the primary means to the perfect socialist state. For citizens it has come to be known, along with Communist Party membership, as the ticket to the good life: job, status, consumer goods and a better future for one's children. Although the Soviet Union, like the U.S., has not been uniformly successful in guaranteeing quality education to all segments of its population (it remains particularly weak in rural areas, and the children of blue collar workers on average are not nearly as well prepared for college as the children of the white collar classes), Soviet faith in the ability of education to transform individuals and society remains unshaken.

In many ways, the Soviet school system is much more rigid than in the U.S. Because Soviet schools are centrally controlled by the state, it is difficult to effect changes in the system. The Ministry of Education in Moscow sets educational guidelines for all schools in the country, and even textbooks and curriculum standards are decided by central authority. Individual schools and teachers thus have little say in what and how they teach their children. This has both good and bad results. Americans who feel that their schools have abandoned "the basics"—reading, writing and 'rithmetic—would perhaps prefer the Soviet Union's emphasis on math, science and language arts. However, the Soviet system does not offer the advantage of such American educational reforms as elective and vocational courses and experimental classrooms and teaching methods.

One emphasis that all schools in the Soviet Union have

that is almost entirely absent in the U.S. is political education. The most important function of political education in the schools is to instill in citizens the values of cooperation, identification with the socialist purpose and respect for authority: Politics per se is relatively absent in the lower grades but, as discussed subsequently (Chapter 11), increases significantly once students enter high school.

A Woman's Work Is Never Done . . .

As early as 1919, Lenin proclaimed that "apart from Soviet Russia, there is not a country in the world where women enjoy full equality." Present-day Soviet officials continue to claim this distinction. However, while statistics show that the Soviet Union has a greater proportion of women employed outside the home than any other industrialized nation, and often in traditionally male-dominated trades and professions, there is still much room for improvement in the status and opportunity afforded the "new Soviet woman."

Economic necessity—both that of the woman and that of the state—has been the major factor in the entrance of women into the work force. The Soviet Union faced a critical labor shortage during its period of rapid industrial expansion, and the country's productivity depends on the employment of as many men and women as possible. In addition, many men's salaries are not by themselves adequate to support a family, so many women have jobs out of necessity or a simple desire to improve the family's standard of living. As a result, ninety percent of Soviet women between the ages of twenty and fifty have jobs outside the home.

Having entered the work force, most women remain in the lower-paying jobs such as teaching, sales and health care, just as in the U.S. To the extent that they have gained greater access to the "male preserves" of law, medicine and science, most women have not seen their careers in these fields progress past middle-level positions.[1] Moreover, among professionals and nonprofessionals alike, Soviet women em-

---

[1] Medicine, which has a high proportion of women, is seen as a "helping" profession in the Soviet Union and as such is of lower pay and social status than in the U.S.

ployed outside the home have a double work load of career and domestic duties that not even an extensive state system of day care and social services has been able to lighten.

To alleviate some of the burden for working mothers, some day-care centers accept children as young as three months. However, there are not enough facilities to meet the demand, and many parents are reluctant to send their children to these facilities before age three. If working parents are lucky, and their apartment is large enough, the *babushka* (the grandmother or other older female relative) lives with the family and helps take care of the children. Unfortunately, the *babushka* tradition is on the wane, so not even this traditional support can fill the void of limited child-care facilities.

To avoid the hardship of two full-time jobs—that of worker and that of mother—many women, particularly among the Slavic population, have simply opted to have no children. This is a source of anxiety for Soviet authorities. As a result, they have instituted some experimental programs promoting childbirth, such a guaranteeing two or more months paid maternity leave and up to ten more months of unpaid leave without loss of employment. Small taxes are also imposed on bachelors and childless couples, and women with three or more children receive a small monthly child-support allowance. Stalin's "mother heroine" award for having ten or more children has also been reinstated, but with little or no impact on Soviet women, especially in the European republics. In fact, an estimated two of every three pregnancies ends in abortion, the most common form of contraception in the Soviet Union. The average Soviet married woman will have six abortions in her lifetime.

As noted, the life of a working mother is not an easy one. The amount of time women spend on child care and housework is so extensive it has come to be known as "the second shift." It is estimated that working women spend an average of six hours per day on housework, meal preparation and child care, in addition to fifty hours a week on the job. Apparently Soviet men, like many of their American counterparts, do not play an active role in household chores, and the arduous life of the Soviet consumer (see Chapter 7) further aggravates the problems a working mother faces during the "second shift."

The Bottom Line: Are They Better Red?

When assessing his standard of living, the average Soviet citizen measures his present life first against what he knew twenty or thirty years ago and second against that of Western nations. As a result, despite the economic stagnation of the last few years, most people are fairly well satisfied with their lives because they see how much progress has been made. Unaware for the most part of the extent of the material achievements in Western Europe and the United States, the average Soviet citizen feels he is fortunate if he has graduated to a private three-room apartment or has seen a son or a daughter go to a university. In the quarter century since Stalin's death, caloric intake has doubled and personal consumption has almost tripled. Even more importantly, after the ravages of World War II, the Soviet Union has been at peace for more than a quarter of a century. Periodic shortages of margarine or winter boots are not enough to dissuade people from the belief that life is treating them well. Soviet citizens have accommodated themselves to such inconveniences, and oblivious to the material possessions they don't have, they're likely to be satisfied enough with what they do possess.

As the West undergoes its periodic recessions, people in the Soviet Union are reassured of the benefits of their system. When acquainted with Western unemployment and double-digit inflation, and the high cost of health care, housing, and university education, Soviet citizens count their blessings in the form of free medical care, low-cost housing, subsidized university education, and a guaranteed job once schooling is complete. They may miss out on some of the high points of the capitalist system, including the breadth of choice throughout the consumer sector, but Soviet citizens are spared some of the pitfalls as well.

While welfare and "the welfare state" have acquired negative connotations in the United States of late, the Soviet Union prides itself on its commitment to the welfare of its people. A large section of the Soviet bureaucracy is devoted entirely to social services, and the safety net it provides is meant to remove as much uncertainty as possible from everyday life. A Soviet citizen need not fear unexpected illness on account of high medical costs; nor must a parent scrimp and save to insure a child's access to a university education. Insofar as the state has had the resources and the inclination to improve the public welfare, the system works. Nonetheless, it is important to note that these services are subject to the limitations of the country's resources, both economic and human, and that it is ultimately the state's decision of what's good for the individual that decides the scope of the service.

From cradle to grave, in those activities that occupy the greatest proportion of the thought and energy of ordinary people everywhere—childhood, education, family life, work, leisure, health—the everyday life of the Soviet citizen is clearly not radically different from that of his or her U.S. counterpart. One could almost imagine meeting on the streets of Moscow or Irkutsk or some growing industrial town people whose life histories and current concerns were no different from those in comparable U.S. cities. That fact alone often seems remarkable to us, given the dramatically different political systems within which we live, and the underlying hostilities that have divided the U.S. and the Soviet Union to the point where each bears the threat and potential for the other's destruction. This commonality is a basis for a shared commitment and concern that we not annihilate each other.

It is not an exaggeration to claim that if their government (or our two governments) would get out of the way, the U.S. and Soviet people would make peace with each other. Rather, it is an observation that, just as in the U.S., there are concerns other than Communist and capitalist ideology and the U.S.-Soviet relationship that dominate the lives of the majority of Soviet citizens from toddlers on up. These concerns point to the desire to go on living in peace as being overwhelmingly more important than defeating the U.S. in a war of weapons or ideology. The instincts for pursuing the commonplaces of everyday life seem certain to be supportive of any efforts by the Soviet regime to reduce the risk of nuclear war, as long as the nation's security is not threatened.

Chapter 7

Where the Consumer Comes Second (to the Military): The Soviet Economic System

The structures and procedures of the Soviet socialist economy are very different from those of the American capitalist system. In a sense, it is like one enormous monopolistic corporation without the governing influence of competition. The overall guidance of the economy and the management of individual enterprise is in the hands of the national government, or "state," as the agent of the Communist Party, using a system of plans of various duration to determine what will be produced and how it will be distributed.

The principal means of production are almost exclusively owned and operated by the state, not by private individuals and corporations. Resources—raw materials, energy, machinery and equipment—are allocated, not by the marketplace but by the state, through a central planning agency (GOSPLAN) at prices set by the state. Finally, the execution and control of the economic plans—making sure that Party priorities are observed—are also in the control of ministries, regional authorities and firms that are a part of the state. Only the allocation of labor and consumer goods in any way responds to market forces of supply, demand, wages and prices, and these areas, too, have the heavy hand of government planners on them. (The supply of consumer goods, for example, is actually set centrally by the government using surveys of demand as only one of a number of inputs.)

The planning of the Soviet economy proceeds from a broad economic plan formulated every five years by the Central Committee of the Communist Party and passed downward through the Supreme Soviet and the Council of

Ministers (see Chapter 9) to GOSPLAN. The economic plan usually defines growth targets and the allocation of investment among the major industrial sectors—agriculture, consumer goods, heavy industry and defense. GOSPLAN then decides the allocation of specific resources among the various industries within each broad industrial category. A set of control figures or preliminary plan targets is passed down through the hierarchy to individual firms and farms to invite comment. After the comments are assembled by GOSPLAN, a final plan is drawn up, subject to the review of the various Party and governmental bodies. Actual operational plans are then prepared on an annual basis.

It is no surprise to learn that the task of planning and managing the Soviet economy from the top is staggering. Literally thousands of different raw materials and manufactured products, together with vast quantities of energy and labor, must be allocated among a comparable number of economic enterprises and kept in balance over both the short and long run. The most important items (including those for defense) are planned at the top, with items of lesser importance being planned at lower levels. In a market economy like the United States, this is done by prices, not bureaucratic allocation.

It is not surprising than in an economy about half the size of the U.S. economy with a comparable degree of complexity and change, planning and execution errors occur, just as they do in capitalism. But lacking the self-correcting feature of the capitalist marketplace, in which shortages and excesses send price signals to buyers and sellers, the plan in its inflexibility tends to be far slower in uncovering and correcting such errors. The result is persistent shortages. The needs of low-priority industries—consumer goods and agriculture—are always relegated behind those of high-priority industries—defense and heavy industry. There are also gluts and mismatching that result from plans, for example an excess of fertilizer or the absence of fertilizer spreaders. Transportation is planned separately, and because it is not given enough priority there is often not the capacity to move products to where they are needed in the most efficient way.

More Is Better: The Soviet Obsession with Economic Growth

Economic growth is a special concern of Soviet policymakers because of the need to support the burden of defense expenditures on the Soviet economy and to "overtake and surpass" the U.S. economically. This latter goal, if achieved, is seen as justifying all the pain and suffering to which the Soviet people have been subjected since the 1917 Revolution. To a lesser extent, Soviet interest in economic growth is stimulated by a desire to raise the standard of living for the Soviet population in real terms, not just in the statistical sense, by increasing the availability of consumer goods, education and health care, and decreasing the burden of labor.

Soviet economic growth from the late 1920s through the 1950s was rapid by international standards, although it was comparable to developing economies in the early stages of industrialization and to other economies in the postwar recovery period. To achieve this growth, the Soviet government brought increasing numbers of workers into the industrial labor force, in part through the collectivization of agriculture (which also made food collection easier); limited the growth of production of consumer goods and food so as to enable more capital to be put into its industrial base; tapped the enormous store of natural resources in the country; and drew heavily on the technological base of the industrialized countries as it added substantially to its own indigenous stock of knowledge.

One distinctive feature of Soviet economic growth is the extent to which it has resulted far more from increasing the quantity of inputs to production than from improving their quality. This means that it has brought into the industrial system more laborers rather than better laborers, more machines rather than better machines, more land and raw materials, and so on. While this "extensive" strategy is quite appropriate for the early stages of the industrialization process, historical experience both in the U.S. and elsewhere tells us that eventually it must be replaced by "intensive" growth, or growth derived from increases in productivity. Specifically, it suggests that unless this quantitative "feeding" of the economy can be sustained—and there are good reasons to believe it cannot—economic growth is bound to slow considerably, as in fact it has since the early 1960s.

Natural Resources

The Soviet Union has vast energy, mineral and land resources, but the best and most accessible have now largely been exploited. Those that remain are, in the case of energy and minerals, in central and eastern Siberia, distant from existing population and industrial centers and enormously expensive to extract and transport to where they can be used. So far, the Soviet government has endeavored to move people to the source of raw materials and to build an urban industrial base there. However, the effort has been hampered by the problems of attracting urban dwellers from European Russia to crude frontier cities located in what are usually inhospitable regions.

Energy, one of the most significant natural resource factors in the economy, appears to have reached a ceiling in its growth rate. Because of the accessibility problem, only coal production is expected to increase at a greater rate than in the previous thirty years. For example, oil production, where the Soviet Union leads all other countries, including the U.S. and Saudi Arabia, will probably grow at less than 1 percent per year as compared to 8 percent in 1970 and 4 percent in 1980.

Labor

There are three major sources of additional labor for the Soviet economy: population growth, population redistribution through migration from rural areas (thereby increasing the *industrial* labor force) and greater participation by the existing work force, none of which offers major promise for growth.

Population growth rates have slowed considerably among the Slavic and Baltic peoples who make up about three-fourths of the Soviet population, in part because of the economic burdens of a family where both parents must work and living space is at a premium (see Chapter 5). Population growth is significant among the Moslem minority groups in the Caucasus and Soviet Central Asia, but they make up only 15 percent of the population. The net effect is that the natural annual growth in the labor pool is expected to decline from 2.3 million per year in 1978 to only 300,000 per year by the mid-1980s.

Growth from population redistribution is no more promising. Large numbers of workers cannot be taken from rural areas without sacrificing agricultural output, and that is unattractive. Further, many of the remaining nonurban population are minorities in the non-European areas of the Soviet Union, with little or no exposure to the culture and technology of urban industrial society and little or no desire to migrate to areas that are ethnically unfamiliar.

Finally, the participation rate is already *very high* by world standards. Unemployment is low and the female labor force is about at a practical maximum, with 90 percent of Soviet working-age women employed outside the home.

Capital

A cornerstone of Stalinist economic policy was the investment, rather than consumption, of a large fraction of national income. (In capitalism, this investment vs. consumption decision is made by firms and households in decentralized fashion.) Soviet citizens chafed at the austerity this Stalinist policy forced them to bear, leading Stalin's successors, including Brezhnev, to gradually increase the *share* of national income going to consumers with an accompanying decrease in the *share* going to capital investment, although absolute investment has not declined.

The Factor Productivity Problem

Productivity refers to the efficiency with which the factors of production are used in the economic system—that is, the amount of output that can be produced with a given level of inputs. Stagnant growth in productivity has plagued the U.S. economy in recent years, and the Soviet economy has been no different. Inefficient use of the factors of production in a capitalist economy is the result of bad fiscal and monetary policy, monopolistic market structures that misallocate resources, or bad internal business management. In a socialist economy, inefficiency arises from bad pricing practices (prices set above or below the level that matches demand with the existing level of production), a misdirected incentive system (discouraging innovation and rewarding misallocation of resources), poor national planning (overproduction of some items, underproduction of others) and, as in capitalism, bad internal management.

In the Soviet Union, economic reform efforts aimed at these problems so far have proven ineffectual. Change involves risks, and as in any highly bureaucratic society, employees at all levels of the economic bureaucracy tend to be risk-averse. Not only does the Party have an interest in control more than efficiency, but too many government officials, industrial managers and *apparatchiki* (Party officials) also have a vested interest in the existing system, either economically or in terms of status and power. In the face of continued unwillingness to decentralize the system of control and frustration in improving productivity through increased efficiency in the use of the factors of production, the Soviet Union has emphasized even more than in the past the promotion of technological progress (see Chapter 8).

The Soviet Economy: Some Sectors Are More Equal than Others

The Soviet economy can be divided into three sectors: heavy industry (raw materials extraction and production, chemicals, machinery and equipment, etc.), including the defense industry; the consumer goods and services sector; and agriculture. In the plan, each is allocated a portion of the nation's resources. Funds are channeled into investment through government allocation of a combination of tax revenues, enterprise profits and depreciation reserves, and long-term bank credit. Individual managers are left with some discretion in how they expend their funds, but ordinarily not over investment.

Heavy on Heavy Industry

Since the inception of Stalinist planning in 1928, heavy industry has been the consistent winner in the plan's allocation of resources, especially defense-oriented branches of heavy industry. As noted above, three factors—stagnant growth (or, indeed, decline) in productivity, limitations on new energy development and the stagnant labor pool—will substantially hinder any ambitious efforts to rapidly expand growth in this sector of the economy beyond the current level.

Guns, Not Butter: The Defense Industry

Not surprisingly, the Soviet government publishes little hard data on the Soviet defense industry and its role in the Soviet economy. Together with the problem of valuing the Soviet force in dollar prices, this makes comparing U.S. and Soviet defense expenditures extremely difficult. It would cost the U.S. about 150 percent or 200 percent of what we spend on the military to duplicate the Soviet force. More significant, what data are available, combined with the observations of Western economic and defense specialists, indicate that the *percentage* of Gross National Product (GNP) devoted to defense in the Soviet Union is about 12–15 percent, as compared to 6 percent in the U.S.

Given the large share of factor inputs—labor, raw materials, technology, R & D efforts—going into capital formation, this means that the low-priority sectors of the economy—light industry, agriculture, social programs and consumption—must be squeezed to make room for defense needs.

Central control of the economy is in part a device for insuring that a high percentage of GNP stays with the military and that the military gets about what it needs to do the job. In a sense, the situation is comparable to the Soviet Union operating all the time with the sort of central priority to defense that the U.S. knew in World War II. Since Andropov assumed control with the strong backing of the military, there is no reason to expect this to change.

Agriculture in the Red

The Soviet Union has only 10 percent of its land area under cultivation, although that exceeds the acreage of any other nation in the world. Fully three-fourths of the cultivated area is subject to periodic drought. Soviet farmland is managed by three kinds of agricultural entities—the collective farm *(kolkhoz)*, in theory administered, worked and owned (receiving the profits) by participating members; the state farm *(sovkhoz)*, owned and run by the government with labor working as employees; and the individual farmer's family plot, usually about an acre in size. The average collective farm has slightly more than 400 member house-holds, 7,000 acres of sown cropland and 3,000 head of livestock. State farms are roughly twice this size, and they are more in number. Both are under control of the Party and subject to direction from above.

While farm productivity has increased significantly, pro-duction problems have plagued the agricultural sector of the Soviet economy from the start of Communist rule and particularly since the process of industrialization and collec-tivization began in the late 1920s. This system has not kept pace with the demands of urban consumers for more, better, and cheaper foodstuffs. Much of the gap is filled either by imports or the family plot, which produces some 25 percent of all food on only 3 percent of the arable land.

Khrushchev sought to remedy the agricultural problem in the mid-1950s with the Virgin Lands program in which, in lieu of making a major effort to increase productivity on existing agricultural lands, millions of acres of marginal land in the steppes east of the Volga River were brought under cultivation. He also introduced various other programs, such as the widespread planting of corn, improvement in prices and related material incentives and institution of cost accounting in *kolkhozy*. The Brezhnev regime continued major efforts to improve agriculture, but results have been unsatisfactory, as drought and other weather problems have necessitated annual grain imports of up to 44 million tons in each of the years from 1978 to 1981. Nevertheless, while the typical Western view is that Soviet agriculture has been a failure, agricultural output increased about 3½ percent per year over the 1950 to 1977 period, the Soviet Union is now the second-largest grain producer in the world (China is first) and no one in the Soviet Union starves.

There are unquestionably basic problems in agriculture beyond those due to climate, but their solution requires institutional changes, perhaps along the lines followed in Hungary, where an effort has been made to measure public demand and decentralize some decision-making without sur-rendering Party control. There may be new willingness under Andropov, who knows the Hungarian experience well, to permit such changes.

Last and Least: The Consumer Sector

To meet their shopping needs, Soviet planners provide consumers with a limited variety of large department and grocery stores, pharmacies, small specialty shops, restaurants and other retail outlets in the urban areas and consumer cooperative stores in rural areas. Prices are set by government planners. This policy creates a retail system that is a nightmare of excesses of undesired goods no one will buy (i.e., prices are too high) juxtaposed against a frequent scarcity of sought-after goods (i.e., prices are too low), especially outside the major cities and in the rural areas. In the latter instance, foreign observers often and accurately picture Soviet consumers as lined up at a store and counters with their *avos'ka* (net sacks—the term means "perchance") where a rarely available but high-quality and affordable item is suddenly for sale. In fact, people will often queue up in a line even if they don't need an item because the line defines a desirable and therefore tradable or resalable good.

Certain consumer goods available to most households in the United States—television sets, radios, cameras, books, tickets to movie theaters and sporting events, and public transportation—are readily available and affordable in the Soviet Union. About one-fourth of all consumption is social goods, which are nominally free—education, health care, care for infants and elderly. Many consumer goods, such as clothing, shoes, meat and fresh fruit, are sometimes available but are costly and of lower quality than in the U.S. Housing is the single biggest gripe of Soviet citizens. If you can get them, apartments are cheap, since rents are subsidized (6-10 percent of income). Food is expensive, taking up 50 percent of the family budget. Finally, such things as quality meat, attractive clothes, automobiles, anything imported from Eastern Europe, foreign vacations (restrictions on travel outside the USSR is the second biggest consumer gripe), high technology gadgetry such as calculators, stereo sets, video cassette players and so on, are generally available only to families in the upper echelons of the government and Party bureaucracy.

There is also a substantial second economy comprised of a wide variety of legal and illegal activities, ranging from reselling of consumer items to bribery of public officials. On the negative side, it injects a note of cynicism and lawlessness into Soviet life. On the positive side, it introduces some of the advantages of private enterprise.

The "Second Economy" Is Black, Not Red

The "second economy" is estimated to constitute *as much as 25 percent of Soviet economic activity*. It is comprised of a wide variety of activities ranging from legal activities such as selling produce grown on private garden plots to moonlighting, reselling scarce consumer goods, trading raw materials and services in the industrial sector, or even bribing government officials.

The "second economy" has a positive side in that it introduces some of the advantages of private enterprise into the Soviet economic system. In addition, it provides communication and manipulation from outside formal channels which the Soviet economic system, like any bureaucracy, needs in order to accomplish its assigned tasks. However, it also erodes the authority and legitimacy of the Communist Party and its ideology both inside and outside the Soviet Union and aggravates cynicism and lawlessness among the Soviet population.

The Soviets Are Hurting, but Who Isn't These Days?

At the start of 1983, a sagging economy was bringing enormous domestic political pressure for a slowdown of the costly buildup of strategic weaponry and other defense systems . . . *in the United States*. This development was indeed an ironic twist of fate, since that is what many high-ranking members of the current U.S. Administration wanted to see happening *in the Soviet Union*. As the foregoing pages indicate, the Soviet economy is not faring much better than ours, although it suffers from a different set of maladies.

The Soviets are facing some difficult problems. The Soviet standard of living has improved steadily and very substantially since 1945. People over 40 can't help recognizing that the system has worked well for them, but in the last eight years or so frustrations have begun to accumulate. As to causes, it has been difficult for the Soviet economy to move from what economists call an "extensive" to an "intensive" mode—from simply pumping more inputs into the economy to improving the quality of those inputs and how they are used. Because it has been difficult, the rate of growth in the Soviet economy has fallen.

Unless there are changes in the economic system, and unless the system is made more adaptive to new technology that will generate improvement in productivity, the slow growth will continue into the 1980s. *But,* slowing growth implies slowing of increases in consumer well-being, and after fifty years of promises, how much can the growth of consumer well-being be slowed? For a political leadership that claims to base its ideology on the superiority of the Communist system over that of capitalism and still speaks of "overtaking and surpassing" the United States and other capitalist economies, the ironies are apparent to all. Moreover, the one economic area in which the Soviet Union has matched the U.S.—defense—could well be threatened by the continuing weaknesses in the rest of the economy and increasing demands from the consumer sector. But unlike U.S. administrations, the Soviet Union has a marked advantage here—the Party and the state have the same absolute control over the economy as they do over political activity and can wrench resources away from other economic sectors for use in defense. Even so, as both sides now confront the drain of the arms race on their economies, it might well be time for them to consider the mutual desirability of transferring resources from defense into consumption and capital formation so that their own economic problems, as well as other worldwide economic difficulties, can be addressed.

Chapter 8

Pipelines to the Future: Military Dominance of Soviet Science and Technology

Marxism prides itself on its scientific character, often using the term "scientific socialism" to describe its approach to everything from elementary school education to satellite development. Yet the history of Soviet policy towards science from the Revolution to the present is one of a regime that recognizes science as an essential ingredient for the development of a socialist economy and society but periodically ignored this need in subordinating science to political considerations, most particularly to the needs of national defense.

The legacy of these policies has been the inability of the country to have both "guns and butter" in the scientific sector; it also handicaps the regime's efforts to devote to military applications the scientific resources it needs for national security *and* meet the scientific and technical requirements for developing the domestic economy to the levels of the West. This heavy military emphasis of Soviet science, together with the burdens of politics and bureaucracy, has forced the Soviet Union to import Western technology. This effort, embodied in such programs as the Soviet–West European natural gas pipeline, raises a variety of issues that have a direct impact on the U.S.-Soviet relationship.

History: Bourgeois Scientists or Scientific Socialists

Before the Revolution, Russian science was an elitist establishment within the tsarist government with scientists having considerable social status and earning salaries 20 to 30 times those of industrial workers. The premier scientific institution was the Russian Academy of Sciences, founded in 1724 by Peter the Great as part of his effort to Westernize the country.

Russian science had an excellent reputation in the European scientific community, but its identification with the tsarist government led to the persecution of many scientists and technical experts in the early turmoil of the civil war. However, the new Bolshevik government soon decided that they needed "bourgeois scientists," just as they needed many of the tsarist-era military officers, bureaucrats and industrial managers. Thus, for the next two decades (except for a brief period between 1929 and 1931 when they were blamed for many of the early problems in Stalin's enforced collectivization and industrialization) there was a steady increase in the power of scientists and expansion of scientific and technical education throughout the country. In 1937 and 1938, the situation again changed abruptly for Soviet science with the arrest, imprisonment and execution of large numbers of notable scientists and technicians, including many working in military-related areas, as part of Stalin's Great Purge.

The German invasion in 1941 and the subsequent need for military science and technology brought freedom for some of those arrested during the purges, but many remained in prison throughout the war, working and often leading military design teams in prison research centers. One notable example was A. N. Tupolev, designer of so many Soviet military and civilian aircraft. Another was S. P. Korolev, who later designed the first Soviet ICBMs and *Sputnik* earth satellites.

Although the war brought some dramatic advances in Soviet military science and technology, it also revealed its inferiority to the U.S. in many areas, most dramatically with the U.S. development of the atomic bomb. As a result, from 1946 onward, virtually all branches of military-related science and technology were accorded the highest priority by Stalin and his successors. Although many scientists and technicians who had contributed to the war effort were released, others remained in the prison research centers, where they were joined by some 6,000 captured German scientists and their families (and the equipment from a

German V-2 rocket plant, together with some 100 rockets in various stages of assembly).

The Soviet Bomb

At the time Truman informed Stalin of the existence of the U.S. atomic bomb at their meeting in Potsdam in the late spring of 1945, Soviet physicists had considerable knowledge about the theory of nuclear reactors and explosions. Spurred on by U.S. use of the atomic bomb and the onset of the cold war, the Soviets achieved their first nuclear explosion on September 23, 1949, well ahead of the predictions of many U.S. scientists. Thanks to the brilliant design work of Andrei Sakharov and others, the first Soviet hydrogen device was exploded on an isolated island in the Arctic Ocean in August 1953, only nine months after the first U.S. H-bomb test in the Marshall Islands the previous November.

With the assistance of captured German scientists and 100 captured V-2 rockets in various stages of assembly, Russian rocketry experts began to develop their own ballistic missile capability in competition with the West, where the majority of the German V-2 rocket team, under the direction of its leader Werner von Braun, was leading the U.S. missile development effort.

While great strides were being made in military-related areas of Soviet science, others fared less well. The biological sciences were dominated by T. D. Lysenko, who rejected traditional genetics in favor of his own theory of environmentally induced genetic change, with disastrous consequences for Soviet agriculture and other areas. Pseudoscientific approaches and political considerations hampered the development of cybernetics, where study and research were forbidden because it was a "bourgeois pseudoscience." This caused considerable delays in the development of the electronics and computer fields. Chemistry, especially organic synthetic chemistry, theoretical physics and mathematics also suffered from political constrictions during this period.

During the Khrushchev era, the heavy emphasis on military applications of scientific research, especially in nuclear weapons and rocketry, continued. Other areas that had been handicapped or discredited under Stalin had their legitimacy, proper control and government funding restored. During Khrushchev's tenure, the Soviet Union achieved a number of scientific and technological firsts, including the first earth satellite (*Sputnik*), first man in space and first shot to the moon. Khrushchev also doubled the number of scientific research institutes and tripled the number of scientific researchers, surpassing the U.S. in the latter category by 1964.

Khrushchev also permitted Soviet scientists to establish communication with their Western counterparts, an unheard-of practice in Stalin's time. This was part of a larger effort to assimilate Western science and technology into the Soviet system, since it was clear that the Soviet Union still remained well behind the West in almost all categories of science and technology, including those with military applications.

Initially, the Soviet Union sought to duplicate scientific development in the West, relying heavily on information published in Western scientific and technological journals. But with the West embarked on a virtual "scientific-technological revolution" in so many areas, this duplicative approach was modified in the mid-1960s. The Soviet Union adopted instead a strategy of purchasing Western research materials and licenses to manufacture research and other equipment. This was in contrast to the Stalin and Khrushchev eras when the Soviet Union depended on the erratic policy of simply pirating what it wanted and could get hold of to help accelerate its own scientific and industrial capability.

The Performance of Soviet Science: An A—for the Military

In recent years, the Soviet Union has spent about 3.4 percent of its GNP on research and development, as compared to the U.S., which spends 2.2 percent of a GNP roughly twice the size. What has been the Soviet performance record?

In military-related areas, Soviet scientific and technological achievements have paralleled those in the West in many areas and surpassed it in some. For example, the U.S. achieved missile accuracies sufficient to destroy ICBM silos by the early 1970s; the Soviets achieved these accuracies in the late 1970s. Similarly, Soviet aircraft technology, especially in fighter aircraft, continues to progress steadily but is still a few years behind the U.S. In the quieting of submarines and antisubmarine warfare technology (important areas relative to submarine survival), the Soviets continue to lag behind the U.S. substantially, maybe by as much as ten years. In air defense systems and antiballistic missile systems, their technology is roughly equal to the U.S., albeit in part due to a much greater investment in resources. Not surprisingly, the Soviets come off best in a comparison of land warfare equipment (tanks, armored personnel carriers, etc.).

The success of the Soviet military research and development (R & D) establishment is attributable to a number of factors:

1. Science in the Soviet Union is not only among the best-paid lines of work but is also a profession that offers the maximum opportunity for those freedoms and privileges that are permitted in the authoritarian state. (A Party career offers comparable advantages, but only after long years of service.) Upon graduation, the best of the young scientists and technicians are recruited to the military sector for a three-year period, after which they can pursue alternative positions, although salary differentials, the best technical equipment and funding and additional "perks" such as access to the best housing and special stores tend to keep them there.

2. Military R & D proceeds in a pull-out-all-the-stops, cost-is-no-object kind of political and economic environment. Estimates of the fraction of total R & D devoted to the military range from 40 to 80 percent.

3. The military R & D effort is better managed than its civilian counterparts, with better planning, organization and control.

4. The Armed Forces are able to impose their desires on R & D efforts, especially regarding matters relating to innovation and production. In particular, the process of innovation, whereby new knowledge is translated into useful military hardware, is far more effective than in the civilian sector, where it is handicapped by the structural relationship between the research institutions and the individual ministries and by the incentive system (see below).

5. Through the Armed Forces, Party direction and government funding, the competitive stimulus of the arms race is conveyed to military R & D specialists.

6. The Soviet military R & D establishment actively pursues the acquisition and effective exploitation of Western

military technology. This technology is obtained in part through traditional sources, such as reading Western scientific journals and periodicals and purchasing nonmilitary products, but it is also obtained through espionage.

The Performance of Soviet Science and Technology

The Soviets have achieved many significant discoveries in *basic* science, even though their inventory of Nobel Prizes does not begin to approach that of the United States or Western Europe. In general, Western observers rate Soviet scientists as excellent, and the size of the Soviet scientific establishment is equal to that of the United States (the Soviet research and development community is actually one-third larger than that in the U.S.). Yet overall, Soviet science and technology are five to ten years or more behind that of the United States and other Western nations, with an even greater lag in *applied* science and technology.

One of the problems of Soviet science is organization. The Soviet Academy of Sciences is exclusively a basic research organization, focusing on chemistry, physics and mathematics. This separation has hindered translation of the results of basic research to industrial and military applications within the various ministries, where applied research activities and laboratories are located. The State Committee on Science and Technology has been created in part to deal with that problem, utilizing a system of scientific councils whose membership includes Academy and ministry representatives. Other major weaknesses in Soviet science and technology include:

- •Party interference in scientific affairs;
- •Inflexible planning, a result of excessive centralization of authority;
- •The stifling effects of the Soviet bureaucracy, rooted in the cultural propensity to avoid risk and responsibility;
- •The preemption of resources by the military, which has first call on the best scientists, engineers and institutes;
- •Resistance to innovation and technological change in the industrial sector, related to rigid production quotas;
- •Lack of technical management and infrastructure for rapid diffusion of new knowledge and innovations;

•Political influence in science, best exemplified by the Lysenko affair; and

•Low diffusion of knowledge within the technical community, a function of, among other things, ineffective technical societies, the absence of periodicals with advertising copy promoting new developments and the shortage of photocopy machines.[1]

The Uncertain Pipeline: Soviet Importation of Western Technology

One major feature of the East-West technology gap is the Russian importation of Western technology. The practice has been going on in Russia almost continuously since the days of Peter the Great and is not particularly unique to East-West relations. It is a characteristic of the process of securing comparative economic advantages in trade and the ongoing historical process by which those societies that lag behind the more advanced industrial societies seek by a variety of means to "catch up" as rapidly as possible.

The channels of transfer of Western technology to the Soviets have already been noted. They include (1) Western scientific and technical literature; (2) purchase of single foreign products to be "reverse-engineered" (taken apart technologically to learn their basic design); (3) industrial espionage; (4) purchase of plant and equipment for direct manufacturing use (turnkey plants, machine tools, etc.); (5) purchase of licenses, know-how and training; and (6) foreign travel by Soviet scientists and engineers. The bottom line for Soviet importation of Western know-how is the impact of the importation of Western technology on Soviety military capability directly, in terms of its use in Soviet weaponry, and indirectly, in terms of the impact it has on the Soviet economy and industrial development.

Selling Them the Rope

Lenin once remarked that the capitalists would sell the rope that the Communists would use to hang them. This the

[1]John R. Thomas and V. M. Kruse-Vaucienne, "Soviet Science and Technology: Introduction," *Survey* 23 (Winter 1977-8):26-28.

U.S. and its Western allies are determined not to do. Through a multilateral organization called COCOM (Coordinating Committee), we have an active program for controlling the export of technology with strategic military potential to the Soviet Union and other East bloc countries. COCOM is an informal, government-to-government mechanism that has no strict legal basis in a treaty and in fact is considered by some participants as nonbinding, making its decisions highly vulnerable to internal strains, as made clear in the split between the U.S. and its West European allies on the natural gas pipeline issue. All NATO countries plus Japan are members.

The current goal of export control policy of COCOM is not the *denial* of technology to the Soviet bloc, except in the case of technologies with direct and immediate military applications, but the *delay* of its acquisition so as to enable the West to perpetuate the East-West "technological gap" and the West's "time lead." Of particular concern is the "technology of the factory," where the West has a substantial lead in large computers (10 years), computer software, microprocessors, numerically controlled machines and so forth.

For the U.S., export control of strategic military technologies involves not just the COCOM list of restricted technologies but separate U.S. lists as well, including that prepared under the Battle Act, now a part of the U.S. Export Administration Act of 1979. Despite these efforts, the Soviet Union has been able to acquire Western military technology. The U.S. and its allies control what they can, but "leakage" of U.S. military technology to the Soviet Union is inevitable, whether through espionage, reverse engineering of industrial commercial products or other means already described.

"Kto, Kgo": Who Will Strangle Whom?

In the aggregate, both in comparison to the overall development and utilization of industrial, scientific and technical knowledge in the Soviet industrial system and in comparison to the utilization of Western and American technology in other countries, the magnitude of technology transfer to the Soviet Union is quite small, ranging from between 2 to 5 percent of Soviet domestic machinery investment since 1960. We often look retrospectively at the export of our scientific and technical know-how to Japan and Western Europe with some regret for having "given away the store," but when we look at a potential military competitor there are additional concerns. We could be helping the Soviets to shore up their weakened economy, thereby enabling them to continue to devote a large proportion of their resources to military purposes, or we could be directly aiding their military technology—in both the weapons themselves and their manufacturing processes.

What's in a 56-Inch Natural Gas Pipeline: The Problem in Microcosm

In the late 1970s, a consortium of West European countries contracted with the Soviet Union for a 3,700-mile pipeline that would carry Soviet natural gas from Western Siberia to those countries. The Carter administration tacitly accepted the project, but the Reagan administration initially opposed it, arguing that it would make Europe dangerously dependent on the Soviet Union for its energy needs and would provide the Soviets with as much as $10 billion annually of much-needed hard currency, thereby enabling it to continue to devote large amounts of its annual budget to military programs. This opposition was rejected by the Europeans, who argued that supplying 6 percent of their energy imports gave the Soviet Union no significant political leverage in Western Europe, that the Soviets were far more reliable a future supplier than Libya, on whom they were now dependent, and that their stumbling economies badly needed the thousands of jobs that went with building $15 billion of pipeline machinery and pipe.

Thus rebuffed, the Reagan administration attempted to stymie the pipeline by embargoing the use of U.S. technology in construction of the turbines for the pumping stations, technology obtained from General Electric, under license to French, German and British manufacturers, as well as other equipment. These European governments rejected the Reagan initiative, arguing that the licenses had already been granted and the equipment manufactured, and shipped the equipment.

Having lost this battle, the Reagan administration sought to negotiate an end to the West European practice of granting the Soviets and other East bloc countries favorable, low-interest loans with which to purchase Western goods, hoping by this means to frustrate Soviet economic development and force the Soviets to divert resources away from the military sector. As of the end of 1982, there had been tentative acceptance of this proposal from the majority of the NATO allies.

Pipeline to the Future

For the Soviet Union, science is not only a symbol of its ideology but a promise for its future. After sixty-five years of sputtering support and obstruction of Soviet science, the Soviet regime appears to have settled into a pattern of strong support for science but with a particularly heavy emphasis on its military applications. This policy has enabled the country to at least approach matching the West in most categories of military hardware and never again fear being in the position of military inferiority they found themselves in in the early postwar period. However, it has left the nonmilitary parts of Soviet science short of funding, equipment and other resources as well as burdened them with excessive organizational and political impediments to development, a condition that could, in its economic impact, substantially limit defense outlays in the future.

PART III
Shades of Totalitarianism: How the Soviet Political System Works

Chapter 9

Blueprint for a Red Society: The Structure and Dynamics of Soviet Politics

"Go live in Russia" is an epithet that from 1917 onward has been hurled on speakers in the U.S. advocating such "radical" ideas as social security, the right of laborers to strike, the hazards of nuclear power and, most recently, a bilateral freeze on nuclear weapons. The clear implication is that the Soviet political system is one in which no sensible American would want to live.

Thirty years ago, at the end of the Stalin era, a general consensus developed in the U.S. around the characterization of the Soviet political system as "totalitarian," implying the near-total control of the society and its citizens by Stalin and the Communist Party. This chapter employs that characterization as the departure point for exploring the structure and dynamics of contemporary Soviet politics—for exploring its significance for how decisions are made that affect the U.S.-Soviet relationship in the nuclear war context and our long-standing assumption that theirs is a system we would not even want to "be caught dead in."

As it turns out, during the Khrushchev era substantial moderation in the Soviet system led to successive challenges to the totalitarian model; others, characterized as "authoritarian" and "oligarchic," took its place. This moderation is one of degree, however, not of kind, and it remains a system alien to the American temperament. Many of the forbidding features of Stalinist totalitarianism, although somewhat transformed, still persist, if only as an "air" or "feel" that almost has to be lived to be understood, a collective memory of the Stalinist era.

At the operational level of Soviet politics, the legacy goes back to include Lenin as well as Stalin. The Party is the all-powerful force in Soviet politics, controlled by the collective leadership of the Party Politburo and Secretariat, who in turn have been dominated for extended periods by the Party Secretary. Whatever its alien nature to an individual reared in the most open political system of Western democracy, the Soviet system has worked, not only to perpetuate the power of the Communist Party but also to deal with the necessary tasks of governing a vast population and landscape.

What's in a Name? Totalitarianism

The main features of the totalitarian model, as applied to the Soviet political system, include: (1) the total mobilization of the human and material resources of the society for the attainment of a comprehensive moral and material goal (pure Communism) that transcends the individual and ordinary goals of a society, such as stability and security; (2) an official comprehensive state ideology (Marxism-Leninism) that is the sole, legitimizing authority in the society vesting the government with absolute power; and (3) no distinction between a private sphere of individual effort and existence free from government intervention and a public sphere where everything—economy, culture, ideology—is mobilized and directed toward the goal.

The means by which these objectives are achieved include: (1) a single, narrowly based party led by a dictator (the Communist Party led by Lenin, Stalin and their successors); (2) a police system making extensive use of terror to control the population (the KGB and its predecessors); and (3) complete control of mass communication, the military and the economy (Party personnel spread throughout the system).

The totalitarian model of society, while it might have been characteristic of the Stalinist era, was seen to have substantial limitations when measured against the reality of the post-Stalin period, in which: (1) stability replaced revolutionary zeal as a goal of the system; (2) human interests and values were being interjected into leadership decision-making; (3) the ideology became less doctrinaire and less focused on the perfectibility of the individual and society; (4) the Party broadened its base in the society and the leadership became more collective and less dictatorial; (5) the system of mass terror was largely abandoned in favor of other less coercive methods of social control, although selective repression remained; and (6) the system of mass communication opened up somewhat to allow more varied information to reach the population.

The Will of the Party: Democratic Centralism and the Structure of Soviet Government

Perhaps the most striking feature of Soviet government and politics is the power of the extra-governmental institution of the Communist Party of the Soviet Union (CPSU). The organizing principle of the Party is "democratic centralism" in which Party leaders listen to suggestions from below but have the absolute authority to impose binding decisions on the Party, government and society to which opposition, even verbal, is not tolerated. As the *exclusive* instrument through which the proletariat acts to transform society in its interests, the Party is to be followed without question as the essential moral, as well as political, institution of a Communist society.

Party Membership

As of 1980, CPSU had 16 million members, 6.2 percent of the Soviet population. Party membership is 43 percent workers, 13 percent collective farm peasants and 44 percent representatives of the technical, scientific, creative, managerial and governmental "intelligentsia." Sixty-one percent are Russians (vs. 52 percent in the total population) and 75 percent are males (vs. 48 percent in the total population). Other membership characteristics include: 50 percent of all people over 30 with college degrees, and 80 percent of all military officers.

Membership in the Party is not open to everyone—one cannot join at will—and the Party screens prospective members closely, looking for people committed to Communist ideology and Party interests.

The Party Apparatus

The formal supreme body of the Party (in theory but not in fact) is the "All-Union Congress of the Communist Party of the Soviet Union," which meets every two to three years. In theory, the Congress elects the Party *Central Committee,* which in turn elects the *General Secretary,* members of the *Secretariat* and the *Politburo.* In actual fact, the Secretariat and Politburo choose the Central Committee and Congress. Moreover, the Congress has no significant decision-making role. It exists to legitimize decisions already made in the Party committees.

The Central Committee

The 300-plus member Central Committee (CC) deals with decisions closer to the operating level of Party policy and action, but because of its size, the fact that many Congress delegates are minor Party members unfamiliar with ongoing Party business and the infrequency of its meetings, Party decision-making is largely delegated to its own policymaking body, the *Politburo* (formerly known as the *Presidium*) and the CC *Secretariat.* However, many members of the CC are responsible for specific spheres of economic, administrative or political activities and exercise considerable influence. Moreover, the CC as a whole must be considered as *potentially* the most powerful political body in the Soviet Union, in case there are disagreements within the Politburo.

The Politburo

Despite long periods of dominance by single individuals, the ideology of Marxism-Leninism gives particular emphasis to "collective leadership." This concept has its formal institutional expression in the Politburo. The Politburo is a 13- to 14-member committee of the highest-level leaders from the Party's national hierarchy. Since the 1920s, the Politburo has been the inner cabinet of the Soviet power structure, equivalent to the White House staff and the principal Cabinet officers in the U.S., plus having supreme legislative and judicial authority.

Historically, there have been periods of genuine collective leadership emanating from the Politburo, for example in the years 1953–55 and 1965–82. But there have also been periods when power resided almost exclusively in a single person—Lenin from 1919 to 1922, Stalin from 1937 to 1953 and Khrushchev from 1958 to 1964. One of the surprises of the period following Brezhnev's death was the speed with which Yuri Andropov assumed position and authority, although by no means does his power imply that he is free of the restraints of the collective leadership with which he rules.

The General Secretary and the Secretariat

The eleven-member Secretariat, the Central Committee's executive arm, presumably also meets at least on a weekly basis, except during the summer months when Party leaders reside mostly in Crimea on the Black Sea. The Secretariat is currently headed by General Secretary Yuri Andropov, and includes the Party officials responsible for overseeing the state political, economic and foreign relations bureaucracy. The position of General Secretary is regarded as the most powerful in the Soviet political structure. The best analogy to the General Secretary familiar to Americans would be a strong President of the U.S. who completely overshadows the Congress and his own Cabinet. (A powerful Chairman of the Board of a large corporation, with the Politburo equivalent to the Board of Directors and Executive Committee, would also be an appropriate comparison.)

Secretaries are responsible for *overseeing*, not *directing*, in a day-to-day administrative sense, specific spheres of operation in the Soviet government and special Central Committee departments, although the line between review and action in some cases is quite thin. Another important Secretariat activity is the *nomenklatura* function—the assignment of Party members to positions in the Party hierarchy and in the higher levels of the economic and political bureaucracy.

Because of the substantial overlap of responsibilities, there is a partial overlap in membership between the Politburo and the Secretariat. Currently, Andropov and four other members of the Secretariat serve on the Politburo. Because the Politburo has "candidate" members—individuals essentially in apprenticeship to become full members—there is additional overlap at the candidate level.

The Semblance of a Formal Governmental Structure

With the overwhelming power of the Party, one might wonder why the Soviet Union bothers to have a separate structure of government, complete with all the features of a British-like parliamentary system—a constitution, elections, three branches of government and an administrative bureaucracy. The question is not without merit, but in truth the separate governmental structure does have *operational,* as opposed to policy and decision-making, responsibility for running the country.

The Soviets

At the highest level of government is the *Supreme Soviet* of the USSR, a bicameral legislative body made up of the 750-member Council of the Union, similar to the U.S. House of Representatives, and the 750-member Council of Nationalities, whose representation is apportioned among the various nationality groups in the Soviet Union. Despite the elaborate election procedures, these bodies mainly rubberstamp decisions already made in the Party committees.

The executive committee of the Supreme Soviet, the *Presidium,* is the most powerful *formal* governmental body in implementing the decisions of the Politburo. Its chairmanship is the most prestigious (though not necessarily the most important) office *within* the government because it is the formal head of state, although until recently the position has been filled by a largely ceremonial figure.

The Council of Ministers

The formal government of the Soviet Union is the Council of Ministers, in effect the executive branch of the Presidium of the Supreme Soviet. Because of its size—over ninety members—the Council of Ministers also has a twelve-member Presidium or "inner cabinet," distinct from the Presidium of the Supreme Soviet, and headed by a Chairman. Most members of the Council are also members or candidate members of the Party Central Committee, and the most important ministers—foreign affairs, defense, KGB and some important industries—are also members of the Politburo.

The Council is the operational analog of the Party Committees, with each Council member having responsibility for a Ministry, an operational part of the government. There is a large number of ministries of government in the Soviet Union, much larger than in the U.S. (Because of the centrally managed Soviet economy, many are economic ministries, in some ways comparable to the very largest of U.S. corporations.)

These ministries, centrally organized and managed, constitute one of the world's largest and most extensive bureaucratic structures. To gain a sense of its size, imagine a single bureaucracy encompassing the sum total of all of our bureaucracies at all levels of government (federal, state and local) and their agencies, plus all the administrative apparatus of private firms from the largest corporations to small companies with a handful of employees, plus an enormous planning and supervisory apparatus that does not even exist in the United States. This gives some perspective on why the Soviet Union has the economic problems that it does and why change will come slowly in this society.

The Will of Some of the People: The Dynamics of Soviet Politics

In the U.S. political system, with the emphasis on democracy, we like to think of "the people" as the initiators of public policy, although in fact most policy initiatives in our society come from various experts within the government or in related institutions such as universities and think tanks, and occasionally special interest groups, such as business. In the Soviet system, it is the Party in theory, and the Politburo and Secretariat in fact, that have responsibility for initiating public policy, although recently Soviet policy initiatives are beginning to parallel the U.S. pattern. However, because of the obvious time and human limitations, the actual decisions considered by the Party committees and governmental bodies are to some extent set by the bodies themselves.

Once the policy agenda has been set by the Party committees, a whole host of forces begins working to advance one alternative solution on an issue over another. Despite prohibitions against any interest groups other than the Party in Marxist-Leninist ideology and constant criticism of factionalism by the Soviet media and Party spokesmen, the public policy process in the Soviet Union is beginning to approximate what political scientists observing Western democracies call the "factional" or "interest group" models.

The major interest groups involved in various areas of Soviet policymaking include the Party *apparatchiki,* the military, the industrial managers, the scientists and technocrats, the regional officials and the security police. However, at times, just as in the U.S., segments of different groups may have more in common with each other than with their fellow group members, e.g., scientists, *apparatchiki* and managers in the agricultural sector. These elements will often combine to form factions that oppose other factions, such as that involving their cohorts in the defense sector— the military, heavy industry, the defense ministry and associated scientists and Party officials. We often refer to the latter as the Soviet "military-industrial complex."

The Soviet military-industrial complex, like its U.S. analog (more recently we have referred to it here as the Iron Triangle—the services, defense contractors and key Congressional committees), is felt by many to enjoy increasing power in the Soviet political system. It is a force that must be won over to any joint U.S.-Soviet initiatives to curb the arms race, a move that runs counter to the trends that underlie their ascendance to prominence (for example, they are given considerable credit for the rapid accession of Yuri Andropov to power).

It Isn't Pretty but It Works

The Soviet political system, while perhaps not the totalitarianism of Stalin's time, is still a strongly autocratic system with a dominant Party and Party elite concentrated in the Party committees and a highly centralized authority structure. Beneath the Party lies the multitude of ministries and a vast organization of bureaucratic government in which the Party, through its extensive membership dispersion, retains effective control. In this Party domination, elite structure and centralism, the current system represents the continuation of a political culture whose origins go back to tsarist Russia.

In its absence of pluralism and freedoms customarily found in Western democracies, the Soviet system is alien to the average American. But the system does work, however clumsily. A vast, centrally controlled bureaucracy can work. Power concentrated at the top means decisions can be made quickly. The bureaucracy below means control is guaranteed but change, for better or worse, proceeds slowly.

Chapter 10

Hearts, Minds and Bodies:
Internal Control
in an Authoritarian State

In the U.S. today, many people are questioning our commitment to the arms race. We can do this openly, taking positions in opposition to our government, without fear of retribution for ourselves and our families. From our perspective in a free, democratic society, we often ponder how Soviet leaders are able to get their people to give so much of themselves to the collectivity of the state. What is it that keeps Soviet citizens from straying from the course, or from collapsing in the face of heavy burdens on the hearts, minds and bodies imposed by the Soviet foreign and domestic policy objectives, including matching the U.S. missile-for-missile in the arms race?

To secure the commitment to the collectivity on the part of its citizens, the Soviet government employs a number of measures of internal control. These measures fall into three broad categories: (1) the instruments of political socialization or indoctrination—the mass media, the family, the schools, the labor unions and social organizations for Soviet youths; (2) the system of prohibition and rewards of a noncoercive nature—organizations that have control over the reward system and can withhold such essential benefits as access to an apartment, vacation in a resort hotel, ability to purchase various good, admission to a university, etc.; and (3) the instruments of coercion—the courts, the KGB and other governmental bodies with responsibility for the internal security of the Soviet state.

The Instruments of Political Socialization and Indoctrination

Political socialization—teaching people the expectations and limitations associated with membership in a society—takes place in all organized and developed societies. In addition to political socialization, Lenin emphasized the additional importance of indoctrination to achieve political and social control, a concept that has been embraced continuously by his successors.

The agents of political socialization and indoctrination in the Soviet Union are roughly divisible into those for initial indoctrination directed principally toward young people, and those for reinforcement, directed principally toward adults. The family, school and youth organizations fall into the former category, the Party and the mass media into the latter.

The Family

It is an article of faith in Soviet society that parents have a "sacred duty to instill in their children from an early age such attitudes as conscious love of the Soviet homeland, devotion to the cause of Communism, honesty, diligence and the desire to serve the people loyally and to defend the gains of the Revolution." Given the innumerable other demands of parenting in any society, and the particular pressures associated with the fact that in most Soviet families both parents work outside the home, active efforts on the part of Soviet parents tend to fall well short of government expectations in the area of political socialization. In fact, the Soviet family—with problems of alcoholism, divorce, juvenile delinquency and many other consequences of working parents—is often the origin of dysfunctional behavior in Soviet society.

The Little Red Schoolhouse

In modern industrial society, schools everywhere are a major instrument of socialization, including political socialization. Such values as patriotism, respect for governmental authority and compliance with rules are a part of the official and unofficial curriculum everywhere, including the United States. In the younger grades, the political socialization process takes the form of salutes and pledges, songs with patriotic themes, historical and fictional stories about exemplary or heroic behavior in service to one's country (and the Communist Party), the enumeration of Communist ideals and the presentation of teachers and older youth organization members as role models whose behavior merits emulation. In the upper grades, there are messages about the dignity of manual labor as an occupation, but these are largely ignored by students whose career orientation, as in the West, tends to follow that of their peers toward high-status jobs.

Youth Organizations

There are Communist youth organizations for all young Soviet citizens from the age of seven (Little Octobrists) through the early teen years (Young Pioneers) on up to the late teens and early twenties (Komsomol), after which they are eligible for membership in the Communist Party. The Little Octobrist organization draws its name from the October Revolution in which the Communists came to power in 1917. The majority of activities for children in this age group (7 to 9 years) is centered in the schools, but there are also extracurricular activities, similar to those in American organizations like Cub Scouts and Brownies, such as organized play and community service outside school.

Induction into a Young Pioneer "collective" or "troop" at age nine involves a symbolic ritual signifying the child's entrance into Soviet society. Virtually all extracurricular activity for young people from nine to fifteen takes place under the auspices of the Young Pioneers—sports, scouting, hobbies, amateur dramatics, dances, special classes, etc. As a part of all these activities, there is continued emphasis on patriotism and socialist values, the Party as the "heart and mind of the people" and the mighty Soviet armed forces.

At the age of fifteen, Soviet youth enter the Komsomol organization whether in school or working. While still in school, membership is almost universal. (Komsomol membership is usually a prerequisite for admission to college.) Requiring student membership not only reduces the risk of political opposition developing in youth groups but also insures that youthful energies will be directed toward socially desirable ends.

At the Komsomol level of the youth organization hierarchy, political indoctrination is intensified. Regular lectures on Marxist-Leninist doctrine and its applications are given to local Komsomol groups. In summer camps and elsewhere, Komsomol members also receive paramilitary training. But the Komsomol also has become something of a tired organization, with much boredom and cynicism among the membership.

Membership drops off rapidly once students graduate, and many of those young people who retain membership do so because it is a base you want to touch for your resumé, much as social fraternities once were in the U.S. One of the main reasons membership falls off is the high standards of public service and participation Komsomol expects from its members. Komsomol members are expected to volunteer their time to help in factories or on collective farms when there is a labor shortage, to give political classes and to join the armed forces in cases of national emergencies.

Party "Agitprop"

Party propaganda is the responsibility of a special department of the Central Committee with a member of the Secretariat in charge.

At one time, *agitprop* activites, as they are known (short for "agitation and propaganda"), were directed primarily to Party members. In the late 1950s, however, Khrushchev turned its focus to the entire population, and by the mid-1960s almost 80 percent of the audiences of *agitprop* lectures and other programs were non-Party members, and some 20 million lecturers were at work.

The major organizational vehicle for *agitprop* is the ZNANIYA Society (Society for the Dissemination of Political and Scientific Knowledge). The society provides lectures in almost any location where an audience might be assembled—public parks, factory shops, club meetings, brigade meetings on collective farms. Often they are presented as part of a larger program of cultural and entertainment events.

The effectiveness of *agitprop* activities as a means of political indoctrination has often been questioned. Since attendance in factories and military units is compulsory and audiences often are captive elsewhere, there is a lot of reading, talking and sleeping going on among those in attendance. Where attendance is voluntary, audiences tend to be heavily populated with retired people.

Mass Media for the Masses

The final element of the reinforcing system of Soviet political indoctrination is the mass media, particularly television, movies and radio. Stalin made especially effective use of movies as a propaganda medium for reaching the masses, the movie fare generally following the style of "socialist realism" (see Chapter 4) with themes of revolutionary zeal and heroic Russian nationalism.

In recent years, the broadcast media, especially television, have become an especially widely used means for propagandizing the citizenry. Centrally controlled mass media unchallenged by any form of competition in broadcasting, press or publishing offers the Party and state the opportunity to reach an audience of millions instantaneously and cheaply, to control the flow of news, to repeat and propagate specifically desired images—for example, of capitalism and U.S. responsibility for the arms race—and to "numb" the audience by occupying the bulk of their time with entertainment interspersed with political images and messages. Broadcast media have disadvantages as propaganda devices, however, because they can be turned off or tuned out by the audience. In the Soviet Union, indications are that viewers and listeners, like the captive audiences at *agitprop* lectures, often exercise this option. Nevertheless, the Soviet Union has invested considerable effort in developing mass media, and of late television, for the propaganda task.

In addition to broadcast media, print media are also highly controlled and employed in the propaganda task. *Pravda,* the Party newspaper, has an edition that comes out in each of the Soviet Union's eleven time zones. It is only four pages long and is filled primarily with long essays of a political nature, such as the need to improve productivity or the threat to peace from U.S. missile deployments in Western Europe. *Izvestia,* the newspaper of the Soviet government, is six pages long and of a similar nature. These papers are readily available at kiosks throughout the city along with easily affordable politically oriented magazines and pamphlets (a 75-page, professionally written magazine on the role of the Soviet Union in trying to halt the arms race, for example, might cost about 10 to 15 cents).

Go Along to Get Along: The Distribution of Privilege

As in any other society, those people in the upper reaches of the Party, military and governmental bureaucracy receive the best salaries and other benefits from the Soviet system. But the system is also *punitive* in the sense that certain privileges that we in the U.S. consider rights of any citizen can be withheld if one's political behavior is unacceptable to the regime: access to preferred resort areas and special stores where the best goods are sold, and freedom to move around within the country or travel outside it. Should the combination of political socialization and indoctrination and control of privilege still not produce the desired behavior, there remain the institutions of coercion, which are ready to step in to punish deviant behavior.

Coercion in the Soviet System

Responsibility for protecting Soviet society against the actions of Soviet citizens and others who might threaten its goals and operations is divided among a number of Soviet agencies, including local militias, the KGB, MVD (*Ministerstvo Vnutrennikh Del*—Ministry for Internal Affairs), armed forces and the Communist Party. Of these, the KGB and MVD are the most important.

The KGB

The KGB (*Komitet Gosudarstvennoy Bezopasnosti*—Committee for State Security) is charged with responsibility for guaranteeing the security of the Soviet state. This responsibility gives the organization authority over border control, security activities outside the country (including espionage), matters relating to foreigners within the country and all "crimes against the state." The KGB is a state committee with the same status as a ministry under the Council of Ministers of the USSR, run by a mixture of Party functionaries and professional security police. Yuri Andropov, Brezhnev's successor, served as head of the KGB from 1967 until 1982.

In executing its responsibility for insuring state security, the KGB has wide-ranging authority within the Soviet Union, with KGB branches in each of the union republic governments and all governmental organizations, reporting to the national KGB headquarters in Moscow. In addition, KGB personnel are placed in all Party, governmental and military bodies, including the MVD, to insure political reliability. The unidentified presence of KGB operatives in these organizations not only stifles "counterrevolutionary" behavior but also stimulates individuals to do their jobs well lest they be charged with trying to sabotage the Soviet state.

One of the methods of control employed by the KGB is terror, an instrumental part of the Soviet regime from its beginning. The Cheka, predecessor of the KGB, performed its first execution without trial in February 1918, inaugurating thirty-five years of intimidation, arrests, trials, sentences, imprisonments and executions, highlighted by the purges of the 1930s (see Chapter 3).

The Camps

The Title of Alexander Solzhenitsyn's famous book *The Gulag Archipelago* refers to the system of camps strung across the northern tier of Russia under the control of the GULAG, the Main Administration of Camps. The camp population in various historical periods is not precisely known, although estimates put the number at between 7 and 12 million prisoners in the 1930s and 1940s. With this large labor pool, the camps were a major element in the Soviet economy at the time, especially in the construction, mining and lumbering industries.

Under Khrushchev and Brezhnev, millions of prisoners were released, leaving a camp population of around 4 million, of which about 10,000 are estimated to be political prisoners.[1] The massive release of political prisoners in the 1950s and 1960s had two significant consequences: (1) it served to disseminate the knowledge of the existence and

---

[1] Some estimates put the number of political prisoners at almost ten times this number, but 10,000 is the estimate of the CIA and is the most often cited figure.

conditions of the "Gulag Archipelago" among the Soviet population as well as the injustice of the system of widespread incarceration, and (2) it was followed by the introduction of psychiatric treatment as a new and sinister means of mental, instead of physical, coercion to suppress dissent.

Some Hearts, Some Minds, Most Bodies

Clearly, the efforts at political socialization, although overwhelming in scope, have been both a success *and* a failure. To the extent that a high degree of patriotism has been instilled, the regime has been successful. It has also been successful in making people general apolitical. This is not a society on the verge of revolt; there is a high level of support for the Party and government and a low level of demands on it. Citizens will therefore rally to support the Soviet government in times of crisis, such as political and economic pressures from the U.S., not because they have been indoctrinated with and now subscribe to Marxist-Leninist ideology, but because neither the citizens nor the rulers make a distinction between the *interests* of the state and those of the individual. Even in our own society, in a time of crisis we expect that individuals will submerge their interests for those of the state, as was the case in World War II. In the USSR, the "state of emergency," so to speak, exists all the time.

Yet we must also emphasize that efforts at political socialization have been a failure in that the messages directed from the top through the controlled agents of socialization—the mass media, the schools, the youth organizations and the Party *agitprop*—have become routinized, boring and often irrelevant. Moreover, alternative private networks of communication exist that supplement and bypass this formalized system. As a result, the Soviet regime has not transformed its people into "ideal Communists," prepared to sacrifice their own interests for "the Revolution."

Chapter 11

A Day in the Life of Ivan Denisovich's Heirs: The Individual Citizen in the Soviet Political System

Ivan Denisovich is the protagonist of the Alexander Solzhenitsyn novel that bears his name.[1] Like millions of other Russian soldiers and prisoners of war, he returned home in 1945 not to his original domicile but to one of Stalin's forced labor camps for "reeducation" and indoctrination. Today, almost forty years since the war ended and thirty years since Stalin's death and the thaw in which the novel was published, political life for the present generation of Soviet citizens—Ivan Denisovich's heirs—has improved significantly, but not to the point where one can organize an independent, grass-roots peace movement, criticize Soviet foreign policy or oppose the latest Soviet missile system the way many Americans oppose the MX.

Not-So-Free Elections

The foundation of the Soviet formal governmental structure is an election process that *on the surface* is similar to that in the U.S.: elections for the soviets are held on a regular basis and are accompanied by all the fanfare but little of the electioneering that accompanies elections in the United States. There the similarity ends. *For all intents and purposes, there is no choice among candidates*. Only the names of those candidates approved by the Party appear on the ballot, although, at the lower levels of local government, not all candidates are Party members. While in the United

---

[1] Alexander Solzhenitsyn, *One Day in the Life of Ivan Denisovich* (New York: Farrar Strauss & Giroux, 1971).

States there is often considerable choice among candidates, many of whom campaign against the existing candidates and policies of the party in power, in the Soviet Union there is no choice of candidates at all. Rather, elections exist primarily as a dramatic occasion for a campaign of agitation and propaganda on behalf of the Soviet system and a public demonstration of the legitimacy of the regime. The idea that an election might be a referendum on an Administration's handling of economic or defense policy, or even that it might be influenced by a mythical missile gap or a public rejection of an arms control treaty, simply would not occur in the Soviet Union.

How You Play the Game: Ground Rules

As policy debates and the ongoing business of the Soviet system proceed, there are certain ground rules that prevail. These ground rules tend to allow for considerable criticism of the government policies and actions as long as those criticisms are not systemic in nature and are offered by the appropriate professional or client group. That is, they cannot be directed toward such fundamental features of the Soviet system as "the leading role of the Communist Party," the principle of socialism, the work of the central Party organs—the Central Committee, Politburo and Secretariat—the wisdom of Marx and Lenin, the peace-loving character of Soviet foreign policy, and so forth. These limitations explain why such actions as demonstrating against the Soviet invasion of Czechoslovakia or arguing publicly that both the Soviet Union and the United States share the blame for the threat of nuclear war are grounds for immediate arrest, and, if continued, imprisonment.

Equally important is the tone and context of criticism, which usually requires the attribution of criticism to other sources, most particularly Western sources. Further, such criticism must be couched in terms of contributing to a better socialism or democratic process, lest they be interpreted as criticism of the system itself.

Finally, some areas, such as foreign policy and nationalities policy, are strictly off limits. Others, such as economic statistics and state, Party and military secrets, are strictly censored. An individual initiative, much less a nationwide grass-roots campaign for a bilateral freeze on nuclear weapons, in that it would imply alteration, and thus criticism of existing Party policy, would not be permitted to occur in the Soviet Union *unless* it were consistent with a Party decision on its advisability; then it would be viewed in terms of its propaganda value.

In sum, public criticism and comment on Soviet public policy is far more limited than in the United States. This fact is without question. But this by no means suggests that it does not exist and play some part in the overall policymaking process. It simply is a matter of knowing the rules before you play the game. Failure to do so, or deliberately challenging them as dissidents do, can have dire consequences.

Voices in the Bureaucratic Wilderness: The Individual Citizen in the Soviet Political System

It is generally assumed by most citizens in the West that because the election system permits only a single party and the Party dominates the government, Soviet citizens have little say in the public policy process. As indicated in the foregoing discussion, there is some room for individuals already within the governmental hierarchy and associated institutions to influence public policy, although except for the upper reaches, the scope of individual influence is very limited. For the individual citizen—the "man on the street," as we like to call him—there are three major avenues of influence, although each is controlled through the Party and subject to manipulation. They are:

1. Feedback to the numerous Party *agitprop* (agitation and propaganda) speakers, whose responsibilities include checking on the effectiveness of policy implementation and discerning what means are needed to head off discontent.
2. Written inquiries, suggestions, demands and complaints directed either to the news media or to government agencies and officials. Citizens have the right of criticism enfranchised in the Soviet constitution as part of the effort to "build socialism."
3. Participation in groups and organizations. These organizations are of four major kinds:

(a) Party organizations, including the Young Pioneers, the Komsomol and the Party itself.

(b) Party-controlled trade union organizations, in which 121 million workers—virtually every employee, laborer and professional (with the exception of the military and police)—are members.

(c) People's Control Committees and other organizations that, like "Citizens' Advisory Boards" in the U.S., review the work of governmental and economic agencies.

(d) Voluntary organizations dealing with nonpolitical matters such as hobby and leisure-time activities. The influence of these organizations can be significant, as when outdoor recreation and wildlife preservation clubs—organizations similar to the Audubon Society and the Sierra Club—become ecological pressure groups.

Wasting Time? The Impact of Citizen Participation

When asked about the impact of citizen political participation, Soviet refugees and observers give a mixed response. There is no question that members of the Party and governmental hierarchy and experts have far more impact than the average Soviet citizen. But this is also true in the U.S. and other Western democracies. Participation of the kind described in the previous section also serves the regime by stimulating mass involvement and citizen identification with the regime, providing policymakers with feedback and serving as a safety valve for citizen discontent. But this, too, is not unique to the Soviet political system, although other societies that do not approximate the totalitarian or authoritarian model do not take it to the Soviet extreme.

If we were to summarize the essential differences in the political life of U.S. and Soviet citizens, we could say in the former that individuals and groups exercise pressure that is recognized as such because politicians and government are dependent in a very direct sense on support from below: if we don't like a Senator's indifference to the threat of nuclear war, we'll vote him out of office. In the Soviet Union, only passing on information and suggestions is legitimate; pressure is out of bounds because decisions are supposed to be the fruits of science and reason, hence in the hands of the elite (Party). Theoretically, information helps make a rational decision, pressure just the contrary. This is why it is strictly forbidden to organize pressure groups *outside* the organization of the Party and state. That is why the hope of some Americans for a spontaneous, grass-roots campaign in the Soviet Union against the arms race is purely illusory.

The Bold Ones: Soviet Dissidents

Perhaps nothing is better known about the Soviet Union in the United States than the existence of dissidents within the population. The release of camp inmates and relaxation of the system of terror after Stalin's death in 1953—Khrushchev's "thaw," as it was known—made dissent an important Soviet phenomenon.

While sharing many common objectives such as increased freedom of expression and movement, Soviet dissent is by no means monolithic. Sovietologists have identified at least five distinct streams of dissent: (1) religious dissent, including Jewish, Catholic, Baptist, Jehovah's Witnesses and other Christian fundamentalist groups desiring greater freedom of worship or, in the Jewish case, freedom to emigrate; (2) nationalist dissent, including separatist sentiment in the Baltic republics, the Ukraine, Georgia and among the Crimean Tatars; (3) neo-Marxist dissent, where demands are made for reform within the socialist model (the Medvedev brothers are the leaders); (4) Russian nationalism, attacking the Communist Party for its oppression and exploitation of the Russian people (Solzhenitsyn is the leader-in-exile); and (5) liberalism, demanding more liberal freedoms from the regime as guaranteed by the Soviet constitution (here scientist Andrei Sakharov is the leading figure).

What does *not* exist in the Soviet Union is an independent, extra-governmental, grass-roots peace movement.[2] (In fact, a recent effort to start such a movement by a handful of people has been quashed and one of the leaders is reportedly incarcerated in a mental hospital.)

---

[2]There is, however, a Soviet Peace Society with chapters in many cities, but like other Soviet public interest groups it is a government-sponsored organization.

The channels of dissent employed by dissident individuals and groups include underground *samizdat* (self-published) literature circulated internally and smuggled to the West, unofficial press conferences and direct appeals to the West. There have been some public protests, but they have been small relative to these other channels, and there certainly have been no massive peace demonstrations.

The penalties for dissent have varied greatly depending on the severity, timing and source of the challenge. During the Stalinist era, dissent would have virtually guaranteed deportation to the camps, if not summary execution. In today's environment, continued dissent usually guarantees KGB harassment and loss of privileges and employment. Should these means fail to change dissident behavior, other means, including deportation (Solzhenitsyn's fate), internal exile (Sakharov's fate) or incarceration in psychiatric prisons or the camps, are employed.

PART IV

Beyond the Border Guards: Soviet Foreign Policy and Actions in the Postwar Era

Chapter 12

Paranoia or Self-Preservation: The Goals and Strategy of Soviet Foreign Policy

There are two features of Soviet foreign policy about which most Americans feel uneasy. One is our long-standing fear, going back to the Russian Revolution, that the Soviet Union is trying to lead a worldwide Communist revolution that would either surround us, as in the domino theory, with hostile Communist states, or worse, include the U.S. in those legitimate governments it would successfully undermine. The other is the more recent fear that the Soviet Union may actually be planning to conquer us by force of arms. Against the first of these threats, we have established a foreign policy of our own, including numerous alliances, and developed a substantial conventional and tactical nuclear weapons capability. Against the second threat we have marshalled a massive strategic nuclear capability and participated with the Soviets in what seems an unending arms race.

It is in this context that we undertake examination of our basic assumptions about Soviet foreign policy objectives, their origins, and how they might be changing under the new Andropov regime.

The Roots of Soviet Foreign Policy

There are two frameworks for analyzing the roots of Soviet foreign policy. The first focuses on the domestic sources of this policy, the second on the external or international environment. The conclusions one reaches about Soviet foreign policy are very much dependent on the choice of framework. Except for the possibility that interest groups can sometimes introduce elements of change, the domestic emphasis leads one to see Soviet foreign policy as relatively fixed and continuous—inherent in the Soviet system and its dominant Russian cultural group; the external emphasis suggests that Soviet policy is much more dynamic, changing over time as external conditions change.

Internal Sources of Soviet Foreign Policy

The major internal sources of Soviet foreign policy have been variously identified as: (1) the ideology of Marxism-Leninism, (2) "geopolitics", (3) imperialist ambitions left over from the tsarist era, (4) xenophobic fears of foreigners, and (5) the needs of the Soviet economy, especially the technological gap between East and West.

Marxism-Leninism

Those observers who believe that Marxism-Leninism has been an important factor in the process and outcome of Soviet foreign policy formulation point to these enduring features of that doctrine: (1) the view that the "normal" and thus desired state of human affairs is struggle, conflict and change, not, as we believe in the United States, peace and stability; (2) the image of its opponents in the capitalist world as innately hostile to the Soviet Union and its political system; (3) the belief that international relations among nations are in a constant state of flux; (4) the belief that the appropriate direction for this change is toward communist society; (5) the need to keep constant pressure on one's adversaries; and (6) the avoidance of risky "adventurism."

In actual fact, Karl Marx offered no prescription in his writings for the conduct of foreign policy. Lenin, however, saw war first as inherent in the imperialist tendencies of capitalist powers, and then, writing in 1919, as the inevitable outcome of the clash between socialist and capitalist states:

> . . . the existence of the Soviet Republic side by side with imperialist states for a long time is unthinkable. One or the other must triumph in the end. And before that end supervenes, a series of frightful collisions between the Soviet Republic and the bourgeois states wil be inevitable.

In the context of this book it is noteworthy that this statement was made prior to the development of nuclear weapons.

Stalin accepted the inevitability of Lenin's "frightful collisions between the Soviet Republic and the bourgeois states" but foresaw an equilibrium developing in which the world would become polarized around the two hostile camps, with neither able to destroy the other. When it became apparent in the early 1950s that the two camps could destroy each other with nuclear weapons, Khrushchev emphasized this equilibrium in the idea of "peaceful coexistence."

In sum, Marxism-Leninism has undoubtedly had some impact on Soviet policy, but it is important to emphasize the danger of confusing Marxist-Leninist doctrine with the beliefs, or mind-set, of the Soviet people and policymakers. The Soviet leaders, elite and the average Soviet citizen are no longer much moved by ideological cant—by the ritualized allusions to Marxism-Leninism. But this is far from the same as their being without perspectives on the world, themselves and us, persepectives that are vastly different from ours. In fact, they have perspectives that matter enormously—the product of 65 years of the Soviet experience (as well as 200 years of Russian history), the orthodoxies drummed into them from youth, and even fragments of a lingering "revolutionary" idealism when they feel they can afford it. This mind-set, as much as the Soviet fascination with military power, is at the roots of the East-West conflict.

Geopolitics

A second internal source of Soviet foreign policy is "geopolitics"—the process whereby geographic characteristics of a country influence its political behavior. Historically, geopolitics emphasizes the country's absence of significant natural barriers to protect it from invasion, and the continuous need to provide military protection for the border areas and settlements as the Russian Empire pushed outward from its Muscovite origins (see Chapter 1). In the modern era, other geopolitical factors came into play, including the absence of good warm-water ports, leading the Soviet Union to continuously look southward for access to the Mediterranean and the Atlantic Ocean; the large wealth of natural resources inside the country, enabling it to avoid the risks and pressures toward external expansion in search of natural resources or markets for its finished goods that are identified with resource-poor countries like Japan; and the desire to create a protective buffer at Soviet borders with potential adversaries, a desire largely indistinguishable from that of regional domination and imperial expansion.

Imperialism

Because the history of tsarist Russia is the history of ever-expanding territory and borders, Russia has long been accused of being an imperialist state. This sentiment was seen to manifest itself in a strong sense of Russian nationalism, rooted in the wars against Napoleon and accompanied by a religious-based messianism. It was especially prevalent among the literate classes, who articulated a sort of "manifest destiny" in which Russia was seen as the successor to the Eastern Orthodox Empire of Byzantium, centered in medieval Constantinople.

The arguments against an imperial dimension in Soviet foreign policy tend to focus on other motives, including the search for adventure (the settlements in Alaska) and escape (many early Siberian settlers were ex-convicts), which accounted for much of the expansion to the east into Siberia, the aforementioned search for agricultural settlements in more temperate climates and the need for a buffer against invasion.

The history of Soviet actions in the twentieth century invites a mixed interpretation. Following the Russian Revolution, the Bolsheviks aggressively pursued formation of the USSR, sometimes against the will of elements in the component republics. With the abandonment of "proletarian internationalism," i.e., world revolution, in the 1920s (see below), Soviet foreign policy in the 1930s was essentially defensive in character, consisting of a series of diplomatic treaties and maneuvers, including the ill-fated nonaggression pact with Nazi Germany in 1939, designed to keep the Western European powers from uniting against Russia.

World War II was a significant watershed in the evolution of modern Soviet expansionism. With the defeat of Germany and the exhaustion of Great Britain and France, the spheres of influence of these and other earlier European powers in central and eastern Europe were considerably weakened. Emerging from the war more powerful than before, despite her dramatic manpower losses, the Soviet Union sought to expand its sphere of power into the region of eastern and central Europe. The fruits of this effort and their consequences for U.S.-Soviet relations are outlined in Chapters 13 and 14.

Xenophobia

Xenophobia—the fear and distrust of foreigners—and an accompanying secretiveness, both rooted in the peasant culture and the lengthy isolation of the Russian people from the outside world, are traits that have long been attributed to the Russian people by visitors from other countries. As that isolation began to give way during the reign of Peter the Great, Russians found themselves looked down upon as barbaric and uncivilized by their European neighbors to the west. This response reinforced the innate distrust of foreigners and contributed to the Russian obsession with buffer states, large armies and large numbes of weapons that characterizes the Soviet approach to national security. However, there is good reason to believe that this view is no longer prevalent among many members of the Soviet elite today, even though it is probably still generally true of the Soviet masses.

The Soviet Economy

President Carter's embargo on grain sales to the Soviet Union—in response to the Soviet invasion of Afghanistan—and President Reagan's brief efforts to prevent the use of U.S. technology in the construction of the Siberia-to-Western-Europe pipeline as a protest against Soviet involvement in the suppression of dissent in Poland point to the fundamental assumption of many U.S. politicians that needs of the Soviet economy can have a significant impact on Soviet foreign policy. To date, however, these economic sanctions have not worked and have been either altered or abandoned.

There are, however, fudamental economic concerns in the Soviet Union that could alter their foreign policy. First, if, as now seems likely, Soviet oil production stagnates in the

1980s, the oil-rich Middle East may become even more of a focus of Soviet activity in the Third World than it already is. Second, the simultaneous need to raise foreign exchange and import badly needed Western technology through sale of its vast raw materials will continue to emphasize the importance of economic ties to Europe and could turn Soviet attention toward resource-poor and technology-rich Japan. Finally, the pressure of the Soviet consumer sector for more and better material goods (including food) *could* force the diversion of resources from defense, with accompanying alterations in foreign policy. This last concern, in fact, is the focus of those individuals who believe the Achilles heel of the Soviet military buildup is the drain of capital, manpower and other resources from the rest of the Soviet economy. But, in fact, the issue is not "guns vs. butter" but "guns vs. investment"—whether the Soviet Union can sacrifice the long-run vitality of economy (ie., growth) to maintain short-run military priorities.

External Sources of Soviet Foreign Policy

The Soviet Union operates within two interrelated international subsystems. It is at once the leader, along with China, of the Communist world and one of the two superpowers, along with the United States. These two external sets of relationships are significant forces in forming Soviet foreign policy.

Who's Number One in the Communist World?

Lenin defined a substantial role for the Soviet Union in leading the international socialist movement. Subordinated to "socialism in one country" by Stalin in the mid-1920s, proletarian internationalism—the worldwide Communist revolution—was revived following World War II as the Soviet Union actively promoted the establishment of a band of communist buffer states in the countries of Eastern Europe favorable to the Soviet Union.

The Soviet Union's position as the undisputed leader of the Communist world went largely unchallenged from 1917 to the late 1950s. Only the Chinese Communist Party under Mao, the Vietnamese under Ho Chi Minh and the Yugoslavian Party under Tito defected from Soviet dominance. All this changed in the late 1950s. The Chinese Party, which—unlike all other Communist parties then in power (except the Yugoslavs)—had attained power largely on its own, began to challenge Soviet leadership of the world Communist movement. The rift in Sino-Soviet relations that grew out of this challenge is explored in detail in Chapter 16 together with the impact of this rift on U.S.-Soviet relations.

Semipeaceful Coexistence: U.S.-Soviet Superpower Relations

The final, and probably the dominant, external factor in shaping Soviet foreign policy is the actions of the United States and its Western allies. The U.S. has led the challenge of the West to Soviet foreign policy objectives and actions, both politically and militarily, since World War II. It is, in many respects, *the* enemy of the Soviet Union, that one country whose very existence has become the rationale for a major portion of Soviet military preparations.

The U.S.-Soviet conflict, and the cold war that developed between the two superpowers, was, in the Soviet view, a natural outgrowth of the clash between the socialist and capitalist camps each led. In the late 1940s, despite the cold war, the Soviet Union began to pursue a two-track approach to foreign policy toward the West. On the one hand, Stalin stressed the desirability of maintaining militancy, building Soviet military power and consolidating absolute Soviet power over Easten Europe. On the other, he continued to affirm the possibility of "peaceful coexistencè" between the socialist and capitalist camps, seeing in "peaceful coexistence" a means of avoiding Western military interference in the pursuit of Soviet foreign policy objectives and interests. It was left for Khrushchev, however, to expand the theory of "peaceful coexistence" and attempt to put it into practice.

Malenkov, who held power briefly after Stalin's death, had given considerable impetus to this view in his recognition of the danger to the Soviet Union and socialism of nuclear war with the United States. Although Khrushchev blustered over Berlin, rattled missiles over Suez and precipitated the 1962 Cuban missile crisis, he retained the propaganda idea (and probably personally believed) that some means of peaceful coexistence with the West had to be found. Thus, Khrushchev began to make operational Stalin's double track for Soviet foreign policy—establishing peaceful coexistence with the West through arms control negotiations, trade and other means would be pursued at the same time as an aggressive posture on various specific issues like Berlin, support for Third World "wars of national liberation" and modernization of Soviet military power.

Khrushchev's policies were perpetuated and accelerated by the collective leadership under Brezhnev, Kosygin and Podgorny after they toppled Khrushchev from power in 1964. But in the Brezhnev period, new developments emerged that would dramatically affect Soviet foreign policy, particularly the Soviet-American balance of power. These included:

1. A change in the structure of the international system from bipolar to multipolar, with the rise of three new, independent power centers in China, Western Europe as a unified bloc under the NATO aegis and Japan, economically powerful but militarily weak;
2. The development of the Soviet nuclear arsenal and that of the U.S. to the point that the total destruction of one power by the other in a nuclear war was a clear potentiality, if not a near certainty; and
3. The achievement of rough military parity with the U.S. and the accompanying elevation of the Soviet Union to the status of a "global" power.

The United States in Soviet Eyes and Over Its Shoulder

It is an irony of history that the U.S., the archenemy of the Soviet Union, also represents a standard against which the Soviet Union measures itself. Having been left out of the path of progress in Western Europe for so many centuries, Russia always felt backward, ridiculed by other Europeans. In the U.S., the Soviet Union sees many features common to itself and desperately pursues equality with us, militarily and politically, in effect as a "superpower." Although Soviet leaders avoid the use of the term superpower to describe themselves, they unquestionably seek that position in the world both in fact and in stature. Today, with its large navy, transport capabilities and long-range nuclear weapon delivery systems, it clearly is a superpower, the military equal to the United States.

The Soviet Union does not pursue its superpower competition with the U.S. without cognizance of other objectives. It continues its efforts to (1) expand its influence in Western Europe while holding the nations of Eastern Europe under political and military control; (2) increase its presence and stature in the Third World, displacing the U.S. and the West in these regions and, where possible, promoting struggles for national liberation and Communist-defined social progress; and (3) meeting the Chinese challenge. In all cases it seeks to avoid a military confrontation with the U.S., which could threaten these objectives.

Chapter 13

Pivot or Pawn: Europe in Soviet-American Relations

Europe. Europe the crucible. Europe, meaning roots to most Americans, meaning two world wars, meaning a rich cultural heritage and a place to vacation and buy postcards. Europe, a place of major importance in the American perspective—and that of the Soviets. Europe, the odds-on pick of many experts as the crucible of World War III.

It is difficult to understate the importance of Europe in the overall perspective of the Soviet Union and specifically in the context of U.S.-Soviet relations. It was to Europe that Catherine the Great and Peter the Great looked to modernize their backward nation. And it was from Europe that Napoleon and Hitler invaded the Russian motherland. It was down the center of Europe that Stalin's Iron Curtain fell following the end of World War II, dividing Europe into East and West and making Europe center stage for the Cold War. And in the late 1960s, it was in central Europe that the cold war first began to thaw, giving lifeblood to détente. Even now, with the issue of nuclear weapons in Europe and the unrest in Poland, Europe remains a major focus, if not *the* major focus, of the Soviet Union, and both a pivot and pawn in U.S.-Soviet relations.

Eastern Europe: The View from Behind the Iron Curtain

There is a tendency in the U.S. to see the eight Communist states in Eastern Europe as a collectivity—the "Communist bloc" or what used to be called the "Iron Curtain countries"—largely under Soviet domination. Six of the eight states in the region are linked to the Soviet Union by economic (Council of Mutual Economic Assistance, or COMECON) and military ties (Warsaw Treaty Organization, known in the West as the Warsaw Pact), as well as under strong political influence from Moscow: Poland, East Germany (German Democratic Republic), Czechoslovakia, Hungary, Romania and Bulgaria. One, Yugoslavia, is "non-aligned" while still Communist. One, Albania, is fiercely independent.

Historically, Eastern Europe has been important to the Soviet Union for three reasons:

1. Security—as a buffer against invasion;
2. Economically—as a market for raw materials and a source for finished goods (a sort of reverse mercantilism that is less important today than in the past); and
3. Ideologically—to show that Communism can spread beyond the Soviet Union, especially into Europe.

The various Soviet postwar interventions in Eastern Europe were brought on because at least one of these three objectives was threatened. Events in Poland are currently threatening all three.

Poland Is No Joking Matter: The Dilemma of Intervention

The limited degree of freedom of operation for Eastern European countries permitted by the Soviet Union since the early 1950s was maintained as long as they did not deviate from Moscow's design for the basic organization of their local economic and political systems. When they did—Hungary in 1956, Czechoslovakia in 1968 and Poland in 1980—the Soviet Union intervened directly in the first two cases and indirectly, through the Polish military, in the third.

The Soviet intervention in Czechoslovakia in 1968 led Brezhnev to enunciate what came to be known in the West as the "Brezhnev Doctrine," defining the right of the Soviet government to intervene in the internal affairs of any Communist state that was not following the path of authoritarian socialism.

The question of intervention in Easten European countries presents a genuine dilemma for Soviet decision-makers. As mentioned at the outset, Poland threatens Soviet security, economic and ideological objectives in Eastern Europe. To fail to intervene when an Eastern European satellite declares its independence—as Hungary did in 1956—or institutes massive liberal reforms—as Czechoslovakia did in 1968—or alters the basic economic and political structure—as Poland did when it legalized Solidarity in 1980—runs the risk of the Polish virus spreading to the other Eastern European countries. To intervene, however, is to admit that the Soviet bloc is not a harmonious family, alienates the people in the other Eastern European states, is very costly economically in that it means that the Red Army must again be brought into use and, in today's environment, threatens the process of détente.

Ruling Communist parties in other Eastern European countries have sought to innoculate themselves against the Polish virus by various means, in particular the modification of their central planning and control systems. In Hungary, for example, almost half the people participate in some measure in the "second economy," some private corporations have as many as 200 employees and the regime attempts to sample consumer preferences. But political control is closely guarded by the Party.

Finally, the cost to the Soviets of maintaining an "empire" should be emphasized. Trade subsidies to Eastern Europe alone are estimated at $20 billion annually, although this by no means has led Soviet leaders to reconsider their hold over the region.

Translating "Ostpolitik" into "Détente"

What came to be called the era of détente accelerated in Europe in the late 1960s with West German Chancellor Willy Brandt's successful "Ostpolitik"—his look eastward toward the Soviet Union to establish political relations between the two countries and other members of the socialist bloc. (DeGaulle and the Soviets claimed it began with the French leader and his mid-1960s policies.) With goals of its own in mind, the Soviet Union was receptive to Brandt's overtures, and the two countries concluded a treaty that furthered diplomatic and economic relationships. (Soviet–West German diplomatic relations were first established formally in 1955.) Simultaneously, treaties were also concluded between West Germany, Poland and Czechoslovakia, establishing a basis for relations with those socialist bloc states.

Détente created special problems for the Soviet Union in Eastern Europe, however, First, it meant that these countries would turn their gaze westward for consumer products, technology and capital, all of which occurred, even though in the short run the hope of Western assistance in throwing off their Soviet yoke faded. However, by no means was it abandoned. Second, increased intercourse with the West could undermine the very rationale for Warsaw Pact unity— the threat from the capitalist West. As a consequence, the Soviet Union adopted a policy whereby it did not smother these contacts with the West but did retain the aforementioned option of intervention should the Eastern European states deviate too far from a Party-dominated Communist system.

Given the complexities of Eastern European politics, it is not surprising that U.S. policy in the region remains essentially contradictory. On the one hand, we want stability. On the other, we want progress on democratization, human rights and national sovereignty issues. Policies advancing one objective—for example trade sanctions vs. extended credit to purchase Western goods—can easily hurt the other. This is the U.S. dilemma in Eastern Europe.

Western Europe: A Soviet Dilemma

Western Europe is important to the Soviet Union for three reasons: (1) as an increasingly important factor in global politics; (2) as a partner with the U.S. in the "North Atlantic Alliance" and its integrated military structure, the North Atlantic Treaty Organization (NATO); and (3) as the front line intersection between "East" and "West"—the socialist and capitalist "camps."

The Soviet Union would like to see Western Europe unified enough to stand up to the United States—something that was not possible in the two decades after World War II—and strong enough to deal with the Soviet Union as a whole, thereby achieving the accompanying economies of scale in economic relations, as in the case of the gas pipeline. However, they do not want it so unified as to have a nationalistic policy such as that of China, representing a revival of the centuries-old threat on their western border. They also do not want it so powerful as to be able to draw Eastern Europe away from the Soviet sphere of influence with comparable guarantees of security and economic aid. Finally, the Soviet Union by no means wants to see Western Europe as a unified political and economic entity, however improbable that might be, acting independent of, and/or competitive with, the United States and the Soviet Union in the global arena.

If the direction of Europe were toward fragmentation—a system of relatively independent states—the Soviet Union would be pleased with the movement unless it included a powerful German state possessing nuclear weapons. Such a move might offer an opportunity for the "Finlandization" of Western Europe (referring to the special status accorded the Finns by the Soviet Union). Western European nations would buy protection with concessions on foreign policy, trade agreements and sensitivity to Moscow in their domestic political affairs, and perhaps meet the long-sought Soviet goal in their respective governments of a role for West European Communists.

Three's a Crowd: U.S.–Soviet–Western European Relations

In the Soviet view, NATO has long been the principal instrument by which the United States has sought to control Western Europe and, more recently, to control détente. The U.S. has been able to exert control over NATO by virtue of its dominance in nuclear weaponry—only Britain among NATO members and France have a significant nuclear capability—and the presence of American troops along West Germany's eastern frontier. U.S. efforts to control détente have focused on controlling American high technology, much sought-after by West Europeans, but as epitomized in the abortive effort to stop the Soviet-West European gas pipeline, have so far been less than successful. The European Common Market is also seen by the Soviets as an extension of NATO, especially insofar as American multinational corporations play a key role in the economic integration. This U.S. leverage over Western Europe cannot be easily displaced by the Soviets, much as they might wish it.

While recognizing the importance of U.S. participation in

détente and their leadership of NATO in the last quarter-century, there is little reason to believe the Soviet Union would want this "leadership as dominance" to continue. As Western Europe becomes more independent, the gradual, but not precipitous, withdrawal of American military and economic influence would be welcome in the Soviet Union, assuming, of course, that it would not be replaced by that of a nuclear-armed West Germany.

Arms Control in Europe

One fundamental question underlying Western Europe's global status is its political alignment. This question has been at the heart of the recent controversy over arms control in Europe. European arms control in recent years has focused on two realms: (1) negotiations on conventional weapons and troops, and short-range nuclear weapons deployed in central Europe (called the Mutual and Balanced Force Reductions (MBFR) negotiations) and (2) negotiations on intermediate-range nuclear forces, with particular focus on the Soviet SS-20 mobile ballistic missile and the prospective deployment in Western Europe of Pershing II and ground-launched cruise missiles capable of reaching the Soviet Union. This latter forum is usually referred to as the Inter-mediate-Range Nuclear Force (INF) negotiations.

MBFR, although largely an American-conceived project, followed in the path of Soviet-sponsored efforts to ease tensions in central Europe through the Conference on Security and Cooperation in Europe (CSCE). MBFR is more narrowly focused, however, and deals with the specific military forces by which security is maintained for both sides, not just the atmosphere or context. The MBFR negotiations, begun in 1975 under President Ford, were suspended by the Reagan administration and are unlikely to be resumed in the near future.

The planned deployment of Pershing II and ground-launched cruise missiles (GLCMs), if arms control negotiations do not succeed, has come as close as any issue to polarizing the U.S. and Western Europe. Predicated on a NATO effort to balance intermediate-range Soviet SS-20s already being deployed in the Western parts of the Soviet Union and aimed at Western Europe, the missiles have raised a variety of issues, including (1) nuclear-free zones in

Europe (a Soviet proposal); (2) the question of the Western European position in a U.S.-Soviet confrontation; (3) the relation of this deployment to overall NATO strategy; and (4) U.S.-Soviet positions in the strategic arms talks in Geneva (see Chapter 19). In addition, it has helped spawn a massive peace movement in Europe.

The European Disarmament Movement

Public resistance to NATO plans to install Pershing II and GLCM missiles emerged almost as soon as the decision to deploy them was made. Anticipating this reaction, NATO governments insisted that deployment be accompanied by a "parallel track" of U.S.-Soviet negotiations on limitations of nuclear missiles in the European theater. This strategy proved insufficient, and a European disarmament movement, broadly based and at times extreme in its protest, spread across the countries of Western Europe.

The speed and intensity of the movement has been variously attributed to six causes:

1. Fear that a "limited" nuclear war might mean a nuclear war "limited" to Europe;
2. The failure of the U.S. to ratify the SALT II treaty and the accompanying deterioration in U.S.-Soviet relations;
3. An emerging gap between the younger demonstrators and older Europeans, including those running the governments, who had witnessed Soviet behavior during the cold war;
4. The U.S. decision to stockpile the neutron bomb for possible future use in Europe;
5. In the specific case of Britain, a major political party, Labour, endorsing unilateral nuclear disarmament;
6. Agitation by the Soviet Union and Communists in Western Europe against the deployment, often portraying the U.S. as the greatest threat to peace in Europe.[1]

---

[1]Ground Zero, *Nuclear War: What's in It for You?* (New York: Pocket Books, 1982), pp. 217-18.

Pivot and Pawn

In sum, Europe remains a key factor in Soviet foreign policy objectives and in U.S.-Soviet relations. The strains in relations between the U.S. and its NATO allies are undoubtedly advantageous to the Soviet Union, and there is every reason to believe that Soviet efforts to promote this rift will continue, particularly on the issue of nuclear weapons deployment. The Soviet Union has significant problems of its own in Europe, most particularly in Poland, where political and economic repercussions could create considerable instability, thus threatening détente in the region.

West European and U.S. attitudes toward détente with the Soviet Union continue to differ, particularly under the Reagan administration. The declining support in the U.S. for détente (in the context of the Soviet arms buildup, Afghanistan, Poland, and so forth) is in sharp contrast to strong support in Western Europe, particularly West Germany, which benefits more tangibly from détente than does the U.S.

These differences are perpetuated by the perennial burden-sharing issue in NATO. There is significant support in the Senate for trimming the U.S. force posture in Europe, both to encourage a stronger European effort and to show displeasure at recent European policies such as the rejecting of U.S. positions on the pipeline and sanctions against the Soviet Union. Though not a dominant trend at present, it could resurface strongly if the West Europeans balk on missile deployment.

Finally, the recessionary economic climate in recent years relates to many of these issues. Europeans don't wish to make guns-for-butter sacrifices (especially when they perceive the U.S., in restoring grain sales to the Soviet Union, unwilling to do the same), and a détente-lubricated flow of East-West trade means jobs in economies experiencing record unemployment.

Chapter 14

The Rise and Demise of Détente: U.S.-Soviet Coexistence in the Brezhnev Era

Détente. The origins of the word are French and medieval, meaning the relation of the tensions in the string of a crossbow, ironically the weapon that the Pope once sought to outlaw as too barbaric to be used against fellow Christians. For the U.S. and the Soviet Union, détente meant the gradual relaxation of the tensions that had dominated their relationship in the post-war era.

Détente began in Europe in the late 1960s, but the U.S.-Soviet dimension was inaugurated in 1972 with President Nixon's visit to Moscow for the signing of SALT I and related agreements. With arms control as its centerpiece, it brought forth additional programs for promoting trade and scientific and cultural exchange. There were high hopes on the part of both sides that détente represented an opportunity to turn the corner on the cold war.

But within a few short years, it became apparent that the two sides had differing expectations of the détente process, and some of the earlier tensions resurfaced. Once again the bowstring stiffened. By 1976, President Ford had disavowed the term, and very soon the interaction of U.S. and Soviet frustrations, disappointments and fears had brought the process to a standstill. With the failure of SALT II to achieve ratification and the election of Ronald Reagan as President, the era of détente was laid to rest.

The Soviet Defense Buildup in the Brezhnev Era

From the U.S. perspective, one of the most damaging Soviet actions in sealing the fate of détente was the Soviet expansion of its military capability during the 1970s, bringing out successive generations of new strategic weapons systems and producing them in sizeable quantities. As a consequence, by 1982 the Soviet Union and the U.S. had relatively equivalent nuclear arsenals and delivery capabilities.

In parallel with its weapons buildup, Brezhnev continued and expanded Khrushchev's efforts (e.g., the Hot Line Agreement and Limited Test Ban Treaty of 1963), to establish a basis for peaceful coexistence with the West. In Europe, treaties were signed with West Germany, inaugurating an era of improved relations in that region. With the United States, the result was a succession of negotiations and treaties under Brezhnev, beginning with the nuclear Non-Proliferation Treaty (NPT) in 1967 and including as major accomplishments agreements to limit strategic weapons systems (SALT I), signed by President Nixon during his visit to Moscow in May of 1972, and the SALT II Treaty, signed in 1979. (Details on these treaties and other aspects of the U.S.-USSR efforts to limit nuclear weapons are contained in Chapter 19.)

The Rise and Demise of Détente

The agreements signed by President Nixon in 1972 inaugurated a brief period of relaxation of U.S.-Soviet relations known as the era of détente. In a curious way, détente was catalyzed not by events in Europe, the Soviet Union or the U.S., but by events in Vietnam and China.

When Richard Nixon entered office in January 1969, the Vietnam War was at the top of his action agenda: 200 Americans per week were being killed in action and draft calls were averaging 30,000 per month. Nixon and his national security advisor, Dr. Henry Kissinger, believed that if they could convince Soviet and Chinese leaders to restrain North Vietnam, the U.S. could honorably withdraw from the war. But would the Soviet and Chinese leaders cooperate? Ironically, at the same time, Soviet and Chinese leaders, spurred on by their long-standing quarrel and recent military clashes along their common border, were looking to the U.S. as a potential source of strength against the other.

There were undoubtedly many factors other than Vietnam and the "China card" that contributed to the decisions of

Nixon and Brezhnev to pursue détente. By the late 1960s, the Soviet Union possessed strategic nuclear forces that were approximately equal to those of the U.S. A limit on strategic forces, in particular on antiballistic missiles (ABM), would prevent a costly arms race and enable both countries to channel resources to internal economic needs, and, in the case of the Soviet Union, toward the pursuit of the various other foreign policy objectives outlined in Chapter 12.

The first of these mutual concerns to bear fruit was in China: President Nixon was invited to visit China in July 1971. Within a month, the worried Soviets extended an invitation to Nixon to visit the Soviet Union.

Nixon's visit to China took place February 21 to February 28, 1972, and at the end of his visit Nixon proclaimed that the visit was "the week that changed the world." The visit did not, however, solve the problem of Vietnam, where the military situation for South Vietnam was steadily worsening. On May 8, 1972, just two weeks before his scheduled visit to Moscow, Nixon ordered the bombing of Hanoi and the mining of Haiphong and six other North Vietnamese ports.

To the surprise of many Soviet experts in the U.S. (but not to Nixon and Kissinger), the Soviets did not cancel the Moscow summit meeting, and it was held on schedule. At the meeting, President Nixon and Soviet Party Chairman Brezhnev signed two major arms control (SALT) agreements, an agreement concerning the "Basic Principles" governing U.S.-Soviet relations and several scientific and cultural exchange agreements. The "Basic Principles" agreement, in that it granted the Soviet Union a status of equality with the U.S., signalled an end to an era of U.S.-Soviet relations that the Soviets characterized as a period in which the U.S. dealt from a "position of strength."

In the summer of 1972, the focus of détente turned from weapons to grain when representatives from the Soviet trade ministry came to the U.S. and secretly arranged for the purchase of one-quarter of the U.S. wheat crop for that year. At the time these purchases were made, the U.S. government—in other words, U.S. tax dollars, were providing subsidies for the export of grain because of the excess of production and the absence of adequate storage.

When the grain deal was first announced, it was hailed as a boon to American farmers suffering under low prices associated with the grain surplus. However, when the magnitude of the Soviet grain purchase became known and American consumers realized that these subsidized purchases were going to raise the price of flour and baked goods in grocery stores, many Americans became irate. In Congressional hearings held on the purchase, Senator Jackson referred to the grain deal as "one of the most notorious foul-ups in American history."

The furor over the grain deal passed, however, as most people accepted the assurances of President Nixon and Dr. Kissinger that the United States and the Soviet Union had entered a new era of peace and cooperation. In October 1972, the two superpowers concluded a comprehensive trade agreement that called for the United States to grant "most favored nation" trading status to the Soviet Union (entitling them to the favorable trade and credit terms afforded most countries). Soon thereafter the Pepsi-Cola Corporation was trading Pepsi syrup for Stolichnaya vodka and thousands of American businessmen were making the long trek to Moscow in search of new markets for their products.

The calm of détente was suddenly broken on October 6, 1973, when Egypt and Syria launched a surprise attack against Israel. Critics of détente at the time made much of the fact that the Soviets would certainly have known of Arab plans to attack Israel and made no effort to inform the United States. When Israeli forces gained the upper hand in the fighting, Brezhnev threatened to intervene unilaterally with Soviet forces. In response, President Nixon ordered a worldwide alert of American military forces. Fortunately, a ceasefire was negotiated and a more serious crisis averted.

While it was clearly not as dangerous as the 1962 "eyeball-to-eyeball" confrontation over Soviet missiles in Cuba, the October 1973 crisis was nevertheless very serious, both as a threat of a U.S.-Soviet confrontation and to the nascent effort at détente. As a consequence, Nixon and Kissinger toned down their pronouncements concerning a "new era in U.S.-Soviet relations."

The ultimate demise of détente did, in fact, begin with the October 1973 Middle East War, although numerous subsequent events and actions by both countries also contributed significantly. On the Soviet side, these events and actions included:

- Soviet development of a new generation of intercontinental missiles potentially capable of destroying the bulk of the U.S. land-based missile force;
- Soviet support for the Communist Party in Portugal, thereby contributing to the fall of the Salazar government in 1974;
- Soviet backing, including Soviet-equipped Cuban forces, for rebels in Angola who demanded and were granted independence from Portugal;
- The 1976-1977 intervention of Cuban troops as Soviet surrogates in Somalia and Ethiopa;
- Soviet actions in South Yemen;
- The Soviet invasion of Afghanistan in the last week of December 1979, followed by the installation of a pro-Soviet puppet government there.

Actions in the United States also contributed to the demise of détente. In 1974, the Congress passed the Jackson-Vanik Amendment, which linked nondiscriminatory trade status for the Soviet Union with Soviet emigration policies. Infuriated by what they felt constituted unwarranted meddling in Soviet domestic policies, the Soviets announced that they would not implement the 1972 trade agreement. The fate of détente was sealed politically in the 1976 presidential primaries when the outcry against it, especially among conservative Republicans, became so loud that President Ford banned the use of the word *'détente'* by his staff. Further, at the Republican National Convention, President Ford was forced to accept a party platform that contained direct and unambiguous criticisms of the centerpiece of the Ford-Kissinger foreign policy—détente.

Having defeated President Ford in November 1976, newly elected President Jimmy Carter, seeking to make human rights a centerpiece of his foreign policy, directed some of his rhetoric on this issue toward the Soviet Union. In response to this and other factors in the deteriorating U.S.-Soviet relationship, Soviet leaders implemented harsh domestic measures on two fronts: Jewish emigration was severely reduced and persecution of dissidents increased.

An additional major factor in the deteriorating U.S.-Soviet relationship was the continued military buildup by both sides—despite the SALT I agreements and subsequent arms control negotiations. The Soviet Union added large numbers of new missiles to its forces while the United States increased both the technological sophistication of its weapons systems and the number of nuclear warheads in its intercontinental forces.

Overcoming these strains in the U.S.-Soviet relationship, in June 1979, after almost seven years of tortuous, detailed negotiations, President Carter and Party Secretary Brezhnev met in Vienna to sign the SALT II Treaty setting limits on various intercontinental weapons systems. Throughout the summer and fall of 1979, the treaty was discussed and debated in the United States. The "discovery" of a possible Soviet combat brigade in Cuba in August of 1979 and the takeover of the American Embassy in Iran in November probably delayed a vote on SALT II, but by the end of the year the point was moot.

In the early morning hours of December 24, 1979, Soviet forces entered Afghanistan, the first non-Eastern-European country to be invaded by the Soviet Union since the end of World War II. In response, President Carter asked the Senate to delay indefinitely consideration of SALT II, bringing to an end the era of détente that had begun in the early 1970s.

In retrospect, it is clear from the series of actions and reactions on both sides that despite the enthusiasm with which both embraced the idea initially, U.S. and Soviet leaders had from the outset, and continue to have to some extent, decidedly different views as to how détente was supposed to operate and what it would achieve. On the U.S. side, U.S. leaders, especially Henry Kissinger, saw détente as a way of indissolubly linking U.S. and Soviet interests in ways that would maximize cooperation and minimize competition between the two superpowers. This was, in essence, a new way in which to "contain" the Soviet Union.[1]

On the Soviet side, Brezhnev and Soviet leaders saw the inauguration of détente as laying the foundation of a new world order in which the U.S. and Soviet Union would divide up the globe and manage world affairs together. Equally important, they felt that this was a stage in the

---

[1] Robert G. Kaiser, "U.S.-Soviet Relations: Goodbye to Détente," *Foreign Affairs*, 59 (1980), p. 501.

evolution of a military balance in which the Soviet Union would never again be militarily inferior to the U.S. or any other world power. The Soviet Union also had short term goals in pursuing détente, including reducing tensions with the U.S. and its European allies at a time when China was presenting a particularly vexing problem to the Soviet Union and opening up East-West borders to the flow of vitally needed technology and capital to the Soviet economy.[2]

The period of détente has now come and gone, and in its fullest only lasted a fraction of the eight-year period from 1972 to 1980. The question of whether it could ever be revived by either party at this point is complicated by fundamental changes that have taken place in the two countries and the world situation. According to Robert G. Kaiser, these changes are the following:

1. Soviet society is far less of a closed society than it was in 1972, giving outsiders a clearer picture of the realities of Soviet social, economic and political life and Soviet military capabilities, and giving Soviet citizens a clearer view of life in the West.

2. The Soviet economy is no longer self-sufficient and, in fact, has become heavily dependent on Western and Japanese technology, capital and, to some extent, grain.

3. The balance of military power has shifted to where the Soviet Union is at or near parity with the U.S. in its military capabilities.

4. Conditions in Europe have changed, with the West Europeans becoming more independent of U.S. influence and the East Europeans moving closer to the West, especially economically.

5. The world energy crisis has put both the U.S. and the Soviet Union in a position in which oil from the Middle East is an important geopolitical consideration.[3]

Handling and Mishandling the Crossbow

For its part, the U.S. record on bolstering détente is decidedly mixed. At the outset, its potential was probably oversold to U.S. citizens by Nixon and Kissinger. With such moves as the Jackson-Vanik Amendment, détente was made

---

[2]Ibid.
[3]Ibid., pp. 502–6.

too much of a political football in the U.S. Nixon's successors in the White House proved unable to decide how important détente should have been as a goal for their administrations when challenged, as President Ford was by conservative elements of his party in 1976 and President Carter was by events in Afghanistan and Poland in 1980.

With the election of President Reagan in November 1980, détente was finally laid to rest. In its place the U.S.-Soviet relationship began to turn backwards in time toward the hostility and isolation of the cold war.

Chapter 15

Side Game: The Soviet Challenge in the Third World

Recent events in El Salvador and Nicaragua; Lebanon, Afghanistan and Iran; and Angola and Ethiopia, as well as in other parts of the globe, have focused attention on the goals and actions of the Soviet Union in the Third World and their significance for U.S.-Soviet relations. They have raised questions as to whether there is some overarching rhyme or reason to the widespread Soviet involvement in these regions. Are the Soviets redefining their role and expectations in the Third World now that they have military power with a global reach? To what extent are Soviet actions in various Third World regions increasing the probability of a U.S.-Soviet military clash there, one that could escalate, following the lines of many popular scenarios, to an all-out nuclear war? In exploring these dimensions of Soviet foreign involvement in the following pages, four main points deserve emphasis:

- The *goal* of Soviet Third World involvement is primarily to gain strategic advantages of a military and economic nature as it pursues the status of a global superpower, and only secondarily to meet its "responsibility" to assist Third World proletarians in their "national liberation struggle."
- The *means* employed by the Soviet Union to achieve its goals have been primarily military aid, and to a lesser extent economic aid, technical aid and efforts to reach beyond the government-to-government interface and establish relations with political parties,

trade unions, student groups, mass media representatives and so on.

- For the most part, Soviet endeavors in the Third World have brought it only *meager success,* because (a) indigenous Third World leaders, while many are socialist in their thinking, are first and foremost strongly nationalistic, and (b) the weakness of the Soviet economy has made it difficult to follow military aid with economic aid, especially economic aid not linked to Soviet goods and markets.

- The *price* the Soviet Union has paid for its meager Third World gains (and failures) has been substantial in that, together with other Soviet actions, they have aroused the anxieties of the American public and government to the point where we have pulled back from détente and arms control negotiations, both of which the Soviet Union wants very much.

A Quarter-Century of Bad Fishing in Troubled Waters

At the time of Stalin's death in 1953, the involvement and influence of the Soviet Union in the Third World was very small. In fact, the Soviet Union at that time had diplomatic or economic relations with few Third World countries. This position was in sharp contrast to the United States and Western European countries, which (a) had extensive relations with Third World countries around the globe, including many existing and former colonies, and (b) deployed military forces throughout the developing world.

Over the next two decades, this situation changed dramatically. The Soviet Union embarked on a program of outreach well beyond its immediate border regions to establish relations with most of the new nations of Asia and Africa. Simultaneously, the Western powers, despite American efforts to create anti-Soviet alliances in the Third World, were losing their influence as newly independent countries sought to maintain their independence of the major blocs.

During the decade of Khrushchev's rule (1953–64), the primary motivation was preemption of U.S. moves in these areas, although this was accompanied by hope that the Third World would break free of the imperialist West and establish their economies on the Soviet model (even though in many key cases [Egypt, Iraq], large Soviet aid programs were initiated at the same time as nationalist leaders suppressed local Communist movements). The fall of Khrushchev and the beginnings of the Brezhnev era coincided with the Soviet expulsion from Ghana, Indonesia and other areas. As a result, the prior emphasis was replaced by a longer-term view of creating permanent ties with Third World countries in areas of special strategic and economic interest, using military aid as the principal tool.

Military aid, more so than economic aid, is seen as a means of rapid entry into a positive relationship with a country because it (1) leads to relations with central authorities (most Third World nations are ruled by their military); (2) can be planned and executed quickly; (3) reduces the dependence of the Third World country on the West; and (4) is believed to be a means of strengthening socialist tendencies among the officer corps in Third World countries.

Soviet military aid, like Soviet economic aid, has been supported by two factors—attractive prices and credit terms. Initially, the military aid program cost the Soviet Union very little, since most of the equipment delivered to Third World countries was obsolete for Soviet defense purposes. But by the early 1970s the Soviet Union, like the U.S., was meeting the buyers' demand for more sophisticated equipment and technical assistance, although it was often insisting on payment in much-needed hard currency.

The Soviet record of success with its military aid program has not been good. Unquestionably, in reducing their dependence on the West, it has helped to make possible nonalignment among many Third World countries at the same time as it has bolstered the Soviet Union's sought-after image of an anti-imperialist power. It has also provided entrée into countries where the Soviet Union had not been before, and once inside, it was able to expand its influence with economic and technical aid. However, Soviet military aid has had some major failures, perhaps the most dramatic being Anwar Sadat's ejection of some 10,000 Soviet military advisors from Egypt in 1972 and his subsequent turn to the U.S. for assistance. The ouster of leftists like Nkrumah in Ghana, despite substantial Soviet assistance, was another example, and similar failures occurred in Somalia, Iraq and Indonesia.

Yet it must be noted that these major setbacks have been at least partly compensated for by expanded relations with other Third World nations in these regions, although many of these nations—for example, Iraq and India—are now desperately seeking to diversify their aid sources.

Soviet Trade and Aid for the Third World

Soviet exports to Third World countries have been geared primarily to arms shipments and the "sales" of machinery and equipment to those countries with economic aid loans. In 1978, these total exports were $8.2 billion. Offsetting imports of $4 billion were primarily in the form of cocoa beans, coffee and tea (43 percent), crude oil and natural gas (20 percent), and industrial raw materials.

Soviet-aid decisions indicate a desire to establish long-term trading relationships with countries possessing targeted materials of greatest value to the Soviet economy. They may also have in mind that these same materials are often of equal or greater value to the West. For example, 86 percent of the $3.7 billion in Soviet aid commitments in 1978 went to Turkey and Morocco by virtue of their location at critical points along two narrow waterways entering the Mediterranean—the Dardanelles and the Straits of Gibraltar—areas of special interest to the Soviet Union. Equally important was securing Soviet access to phosphate deposits in Morocco for use as much-needed fertilizer in Soviet agriculture. Soviet economic aid to the Third World averaged $725 million per year from 1967 to 1977, far less than the West in absolute dollar terms and as a percentage of GNP (0.05 percent vs. 0.33 percent). It has been largely in the form of heavy machinery and equipment for the construction of large projects in extractive industries, energy development and heavy industry. The Aswan Dam in Egypt and the Bhilai Steel Mill in India are good examples. The aid is given on relatively favorable repayment terms, including low interest and the opportunity for repayment with the product of the project, such as fertilizer and steel, so that the Third World country does not have to acquire hard currency for repayment.

Technical Aid to the Third World

Soviet economic aid, like Soviet military aid, also includes provision for Soviet technicians to help operate and maintain facilities and equipment. In 1978, more than 70,000 Soviet and East European technicians were working in the Third World, mostly in the Middle East and North Africa.

Training and education of members of the indigenous population has also been a large part of Soviet technical assistance. This training has taken a variety of forms, including (1) the training of operating and maintenance personnel for Soviet-built factories, (2) construction of schools and training centers, and (3) the education of many students from targeted countries in universities in the Soviet Union. In 1978, for example, some 40,000 Third World students, the majority from Black Africa, were studying in the Soviet Union and Eastern Europe. Obviously, the Soviet educational program is designed not only to develop a cadre of capable local personnel but also to create an educated elite favorably disposed to Soviet socialism and the Soviet Union.

As indicated at the outset, the overall scorecard on Soviet initiatives in the Third World is not good. At least at this juncture, the much ballyhooed scenario of a Third World conflict escalating to a U.S.-Soviet involvement and ultimately to a Third World War is not on the present horizon, although events change rapidly in some Third World regions, such as the Middle East.

Soviets in the Middle East: Paving the Way to World War III?

The Middle East is a good case in point of the success and failure of Soviet Third World policy. Experts are divided on Soviet objectives in the Middle East. One school sees Soviet Middle East policy as primarily defensive, seeking to prevent the region from being used as a military base by the U.S. or as a base from which to undermine Soviet control in the Muslim regions and population of the Soviet Union. The contending school sees the Soviet Middle East policy as offensive in its objectives, aimed at displacing the long-standing British and American influence in the region, especially regarding control over the flow and destination of Middle East oil.

Whatever its objectives, the main thrust of Soviet strategy in the region has been toward uniting the Arab states against what it terms the "linchpin" of Western imperialism—Israel—and its principal supporter, the United States. This strategy has not proved to be successful except for a brief period between the 1967 and 1973 Arab-Israeli wars.

The major roadblocks to greater Soviet progress in the region are:

- The Arab states are already so divided that invariably the Soviet Union has had to choose sides;
- Arab Communist parties have sought their own political objectives, often at odds with existing regimes, and have been totally, and often viciously, suppressed;
- Oil revenues have enabled Arab states to buy Western technology and consumer products outright, thereby weakening the impact of Soviet economic aid;
- Islamic fundamentalists do not understand or appreciate Soviet atheism;
- Arab countries have learned to play the U.S. and Soviet Union off against each other to their own advantage;
- The Soviet Union has been unwilling to expand its military assistance to its Arab friends to the point where they could defeat Israel;
- Since 1973, the U.S. has been able to "freeze out" the Soviet Union because only the U.S. could bring pressures to bear on Israel, a fact recognized by Egypt's Anwar Sadat.

Cairo's break with Moscow is a critical chapter in Soviet Middle East relations. Prior to Sadat's expulsion of the Soviet Union from Egypt in 1972, Soviet military and economic aid to the country was almost $4 billion. The expulsion and subsequent complete break with Moscow in 1976 (1) underscored the Soviet inability to control the Egyptians despite massive military and economic dependence on the

USSR; (2) proved that any Soviet military presence in the Middle East could not depend on Arab support; (3) nullified Soviet efforts to offset the U.S. strategic preponderance in the region; and (4) left the U.S. as the only superpower at hand for resolving the Arab-Israeli dispute.

Within the Middle East area there are two countries in which Soviet involvement or potential involvement is of a special nature—Afghanistan and Iran. Afghanistan has been of special interest to Russia and the Soviet Union since the mid-eighteenth century, when it served as a buffer to the British empire, whose interests extended into the entire Middle East, encompassing the Arab countries, Iran and India (including what is now Pakistan). As a consequence, Soviet objectives in Afghanistan have focused on maintaining that buffer by promoting Afghan neutrality or "nonalignment." Soviet objectives have included "using" Afghanistan to (1) create difficulties for Pakistan, a U.S. ally; (2) demonstrate its "good neighbor" policies (between 1955 and 1979 Afghanistan was the recipient of $600 million in Soviet aid, a "reward" for nonalignment); (3) minimize any provocation of ethnically related Soviet Muslims; and (4) give the Soviet Union a toehold in a vital strategic area. In 1979 the Soviet Union saw these objectives threatened in spite of the 1978 coup in which the Communists seized control of the country. When the new government had increasing difficulty in consolidating its power in the face of strong Afghan opposition, the Soviet Union chose to invade the country, only to find their first use of Soviet troops outside of Eastern Europe since World War II mired in a guerilla war not unlike that which the U.S. encountered in Vietnam.

Iran, like Afghanistan, has been at the center of first Russian and then Soviet rivalry with Britain in the Middle East for well over one hundred years. The Allies shared occupation of the country during World War II—the Soviet Union in the north, Britain and the U.S. in the south. After the war, the Iranian Tudeh (Communist) Party attempted to gain control of the country but was frustrated by U.S. intercession. With the departure of the Shah, the opportunity for pro-Soviet Communists in Iran to once again bid for control loomed large, but their ranks have been decimated by the Khomeini regime. While the possibility of an aggressive Soviet move in the country at this time seems small, there is good reason to believe that Soviet energy needs and the "opportunities" in Iran could lead the Soviet Union to subtler efforts to influence events there.

With other countries, the Soviet Union has had its greatest success in South Yemen and Syria, and lesser successes with Iraq and the PLO, all of whose governments have ongoing ties with the Soviet government through military and economic assistance programs. But prior ties with Egypt have been repudiated. However, the Middle East has been so much in flux in the recent past that even these conditions could change over a short period of time.

In summarizing the overall picture in the Middle East, Soviet involvement is ongoing—in fact, the largest in the Third World—although it remains open to question as to how successful it has been. One measure of the relative impotence of the Soviet Union in the region was the virtual silence of the Soviet Union during the Israeli invasion of Lebanon and expulsion of the PLO, with whom the Soviet Union has diplomatic relations, in the summer of 1982.

All Quiet on the Third World Front

As 1982 concluded, many observers noted the unusual quiet, if not passivity, that had overtaken Soviet Third World activities. The Soviet war in Afghanistan seemed to have reached a stalemate, there were no new Soviet initiatives in southeast Asia, Africa or Latin America and the Soviet Union was conspicuous by its absence of rhetoric or substantive response following the Israeli invasion of Lebanon and expulsion of the PLO.

The explanation for the low Soviet profile is probably fourfold. First, on the domestic front, they are probably preoccupied by the country's pressing economic problems and the consequences of the Andropov succession. Second, they are undoubtedly focusing a great deal of attention on the U.S.-Soviet relationship, which is at its lowest point since the cold war. Third, they may well be overextended, with a substantial commitment in Afghanistan, the worrisome situation in Poland and the continuing dilemma of how to deal with an increasingly independent China. Finally, there has been no real occasion for involvement: the Iraq-Iran war, the Lebanese War and El Salvador all created no opportunity for the Soviet Union. However, one should not draw exaggerated inferences from Soviet restraint in these cases, or from *lack* of Soviet restraint in Angola, Ethiopia and Afghanistan. But, as stated at the outset, and with a disclaimer because of the potential for rapid change in the Third World, that arena, *at this point in time,* seems less likely as the crucible for a U.S.-Soviet conflict than in the recent past.

Chapter 16

End Game: Who Will Play the China Card?

When the Communists under Mao took over China in late 1949 at the height of the cold war, many people in the U.S. assumed that the China card was in the hand of its fellow Communist giant, the Soviet Union. When the two countries had a falling out in the 1950s and early 1960s, we assumed there wasn't much of a card to be played (although we at one point proposed to build an ABM system for a Chinese missile threat that never emerged). Then in the early 1970s, with President Nixon's historic trip to China, we thought we had garnered the China card. Of late, we are more realistic and are prepared to admit that China probably has the card back in its own deck.

Regardless of who has the China card, the dilemma of China is an enormous one for the Soviet Union. Imagine how we would feel if our border with Mexico was 5,000 miles long (it's about 1,000 miles) and behind the border was a government and 800,000,000 people hostile to the U.S., determined to displace us as leader of the Free World and possessing a rapidly expanding nuclear capability targeted on us. Considering our attitude toward Castro and our reaction to the Soviet placement of nuclear weapons in Cuba, the Soviet paranoia about China is quite understandable.

Division in the Communist Camp

The origin of the strains in the Sino-Soviet relationship is in both long-standing border disputes and major ideological differences. The geopolitical roots of the Sino-Soviet schism go back as far as the conquest of Russia by the Mongols in the thirteenth and fourteenth centuries, a conquest no Russian is permitted to forget. Chinese antipathy for the Russians arose in the nineteenth century when Russia seized sizeable portions of Chinese territory in the Far East. But the real source of friction came in the twentieth century when Stalin continuously shortchanged Mao and the Chinese Communists, even to the point of supporting for a time Chiang Kai-shek's Kuomintang army and forcing Chou En-lai to release Chiang when the latter had been taken prisoner by a local warlord.

The common threat presented by the Japanese invasion in World War II led Mao and Chiang to set aside their long-standing rivalry and fight side-by-side, replacing almost thirty years of prewar bloodshed. However, at the conclusion of World War II and the final withdrawal of Japanese troops, the temporary wartime alliance between Mao Zedung's Red Army and the Kuomintang of Chiang Kai-shek broke down. Once again the two armies were fighting for control of this vast country in which one-quarter of the world's people resided.

Stalin held out little hope for a victory by Mao's forces and urged that he seek a rapprochement with Chiang and dissolve the Chinese Communist army. Like Marx and Engels and the Mensheviks before him, his view was predicated in part on the belief that a revolution would not be possible in a backward peasant country. But it may also have reflected a preference for a neighbor ruled by a weak, corrupt government rather than one ruled by a charismatic leader with broad public support who was zealous in his national objectives. Stalin's prediction proved incorrect: in the fall of 1949, Mao triumphed, Chiang fled to Formosa (Taiwan) and the "People's Republic of China" was created.

Following Mao's triumph, the Soviet Union sought to establish relations with the new Communist giant similar to those that they had with their Eastern European satellites. Chinese resistance to this treatment forced the Soviet Union to accede to a series of agreements that gradually established the independence of the Mao regime and led to reasonably satisfactory relations between the two countries until the death of Stalin in 1953.

In 1954 Khrushchev and his cohorts negotiated a new treaty with the Chinese generally favorable to the Peking regime, but tensions gradually began to develop over the Chinese desire to have a greater say in Communist activities worldwide, and especially in Asia. This was coupled with the growing ideological division between the two—the Chinese continuously accusing Moscow of "revisionism," particularly on the issue of "peaceful coexistence" with the West in the face of the threat of nuclear weapons, and the Soviets accusing the Chinese of "dogmatism." As a result, an open rift developed between the two governments.

Beginning in the late 1950s with Soviet unwillingness to supply the Chinese with nuclear know-how (1957) and back them up in the Quemoy-Matsu crisis (1958), the Sino-Soviet conflict flared into an exchange of bitter personal attacks against the leaders of the opposing countries. It also included Soviet recall of technical advisors from China, Chinese claim to territory in the Soviet Far East and Chinese detonation of its first nuclear explosion the day after Brezhnev took office. The two could no longer be contained within the framework of the socialist camp, and in 1964 they broke apart.

Since 1964, the Soviet Union and China have operated as two relatively independent Communist camps, in competition around the world for the status of leader in the socialist movement and at their common border as potential military adversaries. As a result of the Sino-Soviet rift, Communist parties and leaders in other socialist countries were pressed to choose sides between the two. The division on a global scale focused on a number of factors, including (1) the question of which country was more loyal to Marxist-Leninist doctrine, (2) how best to cope with imperialism and the capitalist states, and (3) the appropriate structure for a Communist society.

The American Card

As relations between the two communist giants worsened, each side very quickly became convinced that the other was an even larger threat to its own security than the United States, the leader of the capitalist camp. As a result, in the late 1960s and early 1970s both countries began to seek improved relations with the United States. President Nixon simultaneously pursued complementary initiatives and the result was (1) the evolution of détente between the Soviet

Union and the United States, and (2) Nixon's trip to China and the diplomatic recognition of China by the United States. The world was now going to have a triangular, rather than bipolar, character, or, as one writer has described it, a world with two and one-half superpowers.

The Chinese Military Threat

The military threat that China poses to the Soviet Union is modest by superpower standards—but substantial and growing.

The nuclear threat consists of about 110 medium- and intermediate-range ballistic missiles, most capable of delivering a warhead in the megaton range on Moscow, and 90 medium-range bombers, also capable of striking targets in the western USSR. Clearly the Soviets would risk tremendous damage from these nuclear forces in any attack on China.

The conventional threat on the Sino-Soviet border consists of nearly one hundred armored infantry and local militia divisions, with a total standing army of some three million troops. While the modern Soviet army could probably prevail in any Sino-Soviet conventional war, the current and potential size of the Chinese army is awesome, and any Soviet victory on land would only come at great cost, if at all.

Can Bygones Be Bygones?

In September 1982, a high-level Soviet diplomatic mission paid its first call on Chinese officials in more than three years, the objective being to resume efforts to resolve the long-standing conflict between the two countries. Public statements by Chinese officials indicated that that country saw little or no prospect for a renewed alliance between the Communist giants and emphasized Chinese determination to remain free of any superpower alliances, including any with the U.S. In November, following Brezhnev's funeral, Chinese Foreign Minister Huang met with Andrei Gromyko, his Soviet counterpart, for the first high-level talks between the two countries since 1969. The talks concluded with both parties expressing the hope that "normalization" of relations between the two Communist powers could be restored.

The Chinese Card in Chinese Hands

Against the background of historical conflict in both the distant and recent past, it is highly unlikely that normalization of Sino-Soviet relations will constitute an alliance between the two Communist giants. Conversely, there will be comparable limits on the extent to which the U.S. will be able to exploit the Sino-Soviet rift. Rather, it seems quite apparent that the China card is once again in Chinese hands—if in fact it ever was elsewhere—and the new generation of Chinese leaders will be pursuing a course independent of the two superpowers.

PART V
Clash of the Titans: The Soviet Military Challenge

Chapter 17

Soviet Military Muscle: Strategic Thought and Strategic Weaponry

How do Soviet leaders think when they think about the match-up of Soviet and U.S. forces? Why do they appear so committed to the continuous buildup of an already enormous military capability? Do the Soviets believe that despite the risks of nuclear war, they can take advantage of military—especially nuclear—strength to help protect and expand their position politically?

This chapter explores the concept of national security that, as best we can tell, prevails among Soviet political and military leaders; the military strategy, policy and means (arms, forces and weaponry) employed by the Soviet Union in support of their foreign policy objectives; and the Soviet theory of the "correlation of forces" by which they claim to measure their position in the international environment. When you finish this chapter you will have an appreciation of a nation to which military force is extremely important, a nation that has used military force (and threatened to use military force) with great effectiveness internally, defensively, outside its borders and by proxy. Against this background you will see a nation that is struggling to "mature" in its perception and utilization of military force in the face of nuclear weapons and the dangers of nuclear war.

From Insider to Outsider: Russian Military History

Russian military policy in the tsarist era was remarkably similar to that which prevailed among other European powers at that time. The country sought to protect its goals of modernization and expansion with a system of alliances

155

and a military force centered on a large land army, the largest in Europe from the early nineteenth century onward.

In contrast to the harmony of tsarist Russia with the world order of the period, the Soviet Union in its earliest decades was often at odds with it. Bolshevik leaders rejected the existing system of nation-states and the international balance of power and articulated a goal of a worldwide socialist order. However, that policy did not initially extend as far as the use of Soviet troops to assist revolutionary movements in other countries. Such an effort was made, however, with the Red Army's invasion of Poland in 1920. When it failed, Lenin told Trotsky that Soviet troops should never again be used to aid a revolution in another country. However, the advice was not taken, and in the 1920s the Soviets used military force to establish Bolshevik rule in Soviet Georgia and to set up the first Soviet satellite state in Outer Mongolia. By the late 1920s, the Red Army had been reduced in size from five million to a half-million men and deployed for defense of the homeland.

From 1923 to 1937, the Red Army remained small. In the face of the purge of its officer corps in 1937 (over half of its senior officers were murdered) and the growing power and militarism of Nazi Germany, Stalin took two routes to solving the growing Soviet security problem: (1) a system of alliances that included the ill-fated Nazi-Soviet Pact of 1939 (see Chapter 3) and (2) a rebuilding program that included major commitments to armor, airborne, air force and naval development and production programs. As a result of these programs, and mobilization in 1939 to invade Poland, Finland and the Baltic states, military manpower had increased to 4.2 million men by the time of the German attack in June 1941.

World War II was a trial by fire for the newly modernized Soviet military and naval forces (to say nothing of the trial that the nation as a whole went through in this "Great Patriotic War"—see Chapter 3). Once Soviet forces succeeded in stopping the Nazi advance (a spectacular, if not miraculous, victory), they mounted a counteroffensive that carried them into central Europe. Stalin immediately recognized the potential for expanding Soviet influence in the region and mobilized Polish and Czech "armies of liberation" and internal communist party cadres to facilitate this objective.

In the postwar period, Soviet military occupation, the result of their victory over the Germans on the eastern front, was the key to Communist takeovers not only in Czechoslovakia and Poland, but in Hungary, Romania and Bulgaria as well. Even in countries like Czechoslovakia, where the Soviet military presence was minimal, Soviet military domination of the region provided the essential conditions for the political intrigues and manipulations that destroyed the postwar democratic coalitions. Later, in East Germany in 1953, Hungary and Poland in 1956 and Czechoslovakia in 1968, Soviet troops would be used to defeat "counterrevolutionary" movements that were attempting to lessen Soviet control of those countries. (In December of 1979, Soviet troops would perform much the same role in Afghanistan; and in Poland in 1982 they provided vital backbone for Polish military repression of the Solidarity labor movement.) Thus in the postwar period Soviet military forces came to be used more as a means of insuring Soviet control than as a means of assisting wars of liberation. The Soviets remain as committed as ever to supporting wars of national liberation, although they seek to do so with military aid, not with their own troops (see Chapter 15).

The Soviet Concept of Security

Successive generations of Soviet leaders have sought to define the security requirements of the Soviet Union in varied ways. Security is at once a state of mind and a set of policies and programs designed to achieve a desired sense of security. In the absence of access to policy deliberations and documentation, very little is known to the outside world of the actual state of mind of Soviet leaders, now or in the past—and thus we are left with the difficult task of inferring their perspectives from objective actions and facts, and from published materials and sources, however, imperfect those resources may be.

In the face of failure and frustration with pre-war and wartime alliances, Stalin sought security in the strength of the Red Army and the transformation of adjacent states to a political model consistent with the Soviet system, not just as a military buffer but as an ideological buffer as well. The problem, of course, was that Stalin's concept of security for the Soviet Union was inconsistent with security for others, especially the countries of Western Europe.

Khrushchev, who assumed the Soviet leadership in 1954, developed a concept of security that seemed to rely less heavily on military force. It included, in addition to a continuous modernization of military forces, especially missiles and nuclear weapons, (1) de-Stalinization and the relaxation of terror internal to the country; (2) an effort to control Eastern Europe institutionally through economic and military (Warsaw Pact) ties and by occasional appeals to common ideology rather than by force (a policy that clearly had its failures); (3) the articulation and pursuit of the concept of "peaceful coexistence" with the West; and (4) a system of Third World military assistance designed to project Soviet influence beyond its border regions.

As a result of Khrushchev's broadened definition of what constituted and contributed to the security of the Party and state, by the mid-1960s the Soviet Union was more secure from attack than it had been at any time in its almost fifty-year history. It possessed a retaliatory nuclear capability, relatively secure borders, control of buffer states in Eastern Europe and had been able to advance its interest to some degree into the Third World without prompting a military reaction from the U.S. against the Soviet homeland.

In the Brezhnev period, the Soviet concept of security came to focus on achieving "equality" with the U.S. both politically and militarily. This translated to security equal to that of the U.S. and a willingness to enter into agreements on a balance of military forces with its principal superpower adversary, principally by means of negotiation. Thus, Soviet pursuit of arms control agreements saw those agreements as a means of improving the security of the USSR. In these negotiations, the Soviet Union often argued that their larger land mass and more numerous external enemies required they be militarily *stronger* than the U.S. in order to achieve *equal* security.

In the presence of arms control agreements, the Soviet Union was determined to continue to build its military forces to meet the threats its leaders perceived in a hostile world from the U.S., U.S. allies and China. But the Soviet pursuit of arms control was also buttressed by their belief that the "correlation of forces" was moving substantially in their favor, and that the relaxation of tensions with the U.S. and the West in the near term—through arms control, trade, scientific exchange and other elements of détente—would augur well for Soviet security and other objectives in the long run.

Sootnoshenie sil: The "Correlation of Forces"·

One of the essential factors in the Soviet formulation of foreign and military policy is what Russian theoreticians call *sootnoshenie sil,* the "correlation of forces." The term refers to the capability of contending forces to intimidate as well as inflict damage on each other, and includes (1) military forces, the primary component, (2) population and economic factors, and (3) qualitative factors such as fighting spirit, cultural parameters and the calibre of national leadership.

In the late 1960s, the Soviets attributed the willingness of the U.S. to recognize the Soviet Union as an equal partner in the world arena and enter into SALT I & II to favorable trends in the correlation of forces particularly associated with their growing military power. Analysis of the correlation of forces with regard to the U.S. may also have led Soviet leaders to conclude that it could exploit the internal disarray in the United States following the Vietnam War and Watergate without provoking a new arms race. Until the election of Ronald Reagan, they were correct in this assessment.

Even before the inauguration of significant increases in U.S. defense budgets in 1978, official Soviet pronouncements indicated a fear that trends in the correlation of forces could be changed significantly if not reversed by (1) reallocation of the awesome U.S. scientific, technological, industrial and economic resources for the buildup of military power and (2) by a political reorientation in U.S. foreign policy, e.g., toward closer relations with China, improved relations with NATO allies and an overall commitment to reestablishing the U.S. as the single global power.

Some observers see a contradiction in the apparent Soviet projection that the global correlation of forces was moving favorably for them (and the potential for Soviet superiority that implied) on the one hand, and on the other the frequent

Soviet assertion that approximate equality or parity in military and strategic forces is sufficient for their defense needs, while it is the U.S. that is striving to achieve superiority. However, it simply is a difference of time frame: the Soviets believe temporary midterm gains or reversals are possible, even though the long-term outcomes are largely captive of historical forces.

One incident that conveyed clearly the Soviet sense of the historical inevitability of the long-term trends in the correlation of forces took place at the signing of the SALT II Treaty in 1979 in Vienna. When President Carter complained about Soviet and Cuban activities in Africa, Brezhnev responded (as Soviet leaders have done so frequently since 1917) with a reference to the "objective course of history" over which, by implication, neither the U.S. nor the Soviet Union could have significant control. Thus, explaining away much of its overseas activities in terms of historical processes, which it does not control, the Soviet Union seeks to rationalize to the West its conscious actions. By this same means it seeks to dismiss any assertion of a "Soviet threat" to U.S. interests around the globe by arguing that while "socialism" constitutes a threat to capitalism, the Soviet Union does not constitute a threat to the U.S.

The Best Defense Is a Good Offense:
Soviet Military Policy

In the Soviet Union, considerable attention is devoted to the articulation of an official "Soviet military doctrine." This doctrine, which identifies the "character of the modern war and military tasks facing the state, and also the methods of resolving them," is drawn up by key military, Party and governmental leaders and then approved by the Central Committee of the Party.

A great deal of emphasis is given to "offense" as opposed to "defense" in official Soviet military doctrine. With regard to nuclear war, Soviet political leaders in recent years have consistently played down offensive doctrine, asserting that they will not be the first to use nuclear weapons. However, Soviet "no first use" claims do not preclude Soviet military doctrine from emphasis on developing a capability of waging nuclear war.

As one moves from the level of military doctrine to the more specific matters relating to military strategy, policy and tactics, Soviet military concerns move to the standard problems of matching military actions to political goals, analysis of the military potential of other countries, combat operations and the importance of various military means in different kinds of military situations. In this respect, the Soviet commitment to a "scientific" approach to military matters, while retaining a distinctively strategic perspective, gives rise to weapon systems and force structures similar to that of the U.S. For example, the two have much in common in that both employ a "triad" of strategic forces—ICBMs, SLBMs and bombers—although allocations to each leg differ (partly due to geopolitical factors, e.g., Soviet land mass, few warm-water ports). One notable exception is the large Soviet air defense system. In contrast, we feel air defenses are too "leaky" (unreliable) and difficult to justify in an environment where neither side is permitted (by the 1972 SALT I ABM Treaty) a significant defense against ballistic missiles.

What They've Got: The Soviet Military Arsenal

In the spring of 1981, the U.S. Department of Defense published a 100-page document entitled *Soviet Military Power,* outlining the buildup of Soviet military forces of all types over the previous quarter-century and emphasizing the growing threat that these forces represented to the United States and the rest of the "free world." (This was to some degree an advocacy document that should be compared with other sources, for example the London International Institute of Strategic Studies annual report, *The Military Balance.)* The highlights included the following.

Soviet Strategic Forces

Over the past twenty years, the Soviet Union has devoted considerable resources to its strategic forces, including:

- Development and deployment of new intercontinental ballistic missiles (ICBMs), many with MIRVed warheads, including the SS-17, SS-18 and SS-19. The

SS-18 can carry 8 to 10 warheads each with a 60 percent or better chance of destroying a U.S. Minuteman ICBM silo.

- Development and deployment of new nuclear-powered ballistic missile submarines (SSBNs) equipped with modern submarine-launched ballistic missiles (SLBMs), including the Typhoon-class submarine (their newest SSBN) and the Yankee and Delta models.
- Continued research on antiballistic missile (ABM) systems. Development and deployment of an antisatellite (ASAT) system, although the threat it presents to U.S. satellites is limited at present.
- The construction of deep, hard, urban shelters and numerous relocation sites as a part of a civil defense program estimated to cost $2 billion annually and focused on maximizing the survival of the government and officials down to the local level in case of nuclear attack. (Little has been done, however, to provide physical protection of industrial facilities or the bulk of the population.)

The summary impact of these developments in Soviet strategic military capability with a more detailed comparison of U.S. and Soviet force structures is presented in Appendix 2.

Soviet Theater Forces

Over the past fifteen years, the Soviets have steadily expanded and upgraded their theater forces, especially in the European theater. This effort has included:

- Modernization and deployment of long-range missile and air forces, such as the SS-20 mobile MIRVed nuclear warhead Intermediate Range Ballistic Missile (IRBM) and the Backfire bomber.
- Modernization, through increased flexibility, mobility and firepower, of Soviet ground forces, including equipping these forces with new tanks, tactical nuclear weapons, surface-to-surface missiles and C^3 (command, control and communications) capabilities;

improved tactical aviation capabilities including new fighters, fighter-bombers, transports, helicopters and reconnaissance units. Among the most modern of these weapon systems are the MiG-21 (Fishbed), MiG-23 (Flogger), and MiG-25 (Foxbat) aircraft.

- Transformation of the Soviet navy from essentially a coastal defense force to an oceangoing force designed to extend the military capability of the Soviet Union a considerable distance beyond its borders, including the KIEV-class aircraft carrier, guided-missile cruisers, attack submarines, cruise missile submarines, new naval aviation and amphibious assault forces.

How Scared Should We Be?

So what does this all come to? At a minimum, one must acknowledge that the Soviet Union has the capability to wreak havoc on, if not destroy, the U.S. in the event of a nuclear war. But that capability does not translate to intention. (If it did, we would be tarred with the same brush.) However, the substantive question is whether the Soviets believe that, despite the accompanying risks of nuclear war, they can take advantage of military—especially nuclear—strength politically to help accelerate trends in the correlation of forces, which they see in their favor.

Whether we like it or not, the *Soviet* concept of security and their more extensive security needs demand at least the rough level of weapons parity with the U.S. they have now achieved. In the short run, neither the reality of the U.S. retaliatory capability, nor the record of past Soviet behavior, suggests they are about to risk or perpetrate a nuclear war with the U.S. However, they are willing to bear some risk of confrontation in hopes of accelerating the "correlation of forces."

In the next chapter, we take a more detailed look at the Soviet view of nuclear war and nuclear war prevention. In the following two chapters, we look first at the history of U.S.-Soviet arms control efforts and then at the future prospects for such efforts, given prevailing concepts of deterrence and the record of arms control to date.

Chapter 18

Dogma of the High Priests: Nuclear War Doctrine in U.S. and Soviet Perspective

What is the Soviet nuclear war doctrine—its policy towards preventing nuclear war, fighting it, winning it, controlling it and so forth? At least 50 percent (and maybe 90 percent) of what you need to know about this question can be gleaned from the following two-step process:

(1) Ask yourself what U.S. nuclear war doctrine is;
(2) In the likely event you are not satisfied with the answer (if you got an answer at all), try asking at least two "experts" (say Congressmen, military officers, members of the national security "priesthood") what U.S. nuclear war doctrine is.

If any two "experts" give you the same answer it will be a miracle. Today, U.S. nuclear war doctrine is as ill-defined as that of the Soviet Union—and probably about as relevant as an examination of today's Soviet nuclear war doctrine, which is to say it is interesting but does not appear to drive the problem of the nuclear arms race, deteriorating U.S.-Soviet relations, nuclear proliferation, prolific conventional arms sales to the Third World or any of the other major issues associated with preventing nuclear war.

Doctrine and Priesthoods

It is no accident that the term "doctrine" (which the Soviets like to use) and the term "priesthood" are used to characterize U.S. and Soviet pronouncements on policy toward nuclear war—and the community that holds forth on such issues. Nuclear doctrine has progressed far beyond the simple schoolyard concept of deterrence—"If you hit me or one of my friends, I'll hit you back, and, if possible, harder"—to a language and logic beyond the grasp of both the lay audience and Presidents. To be sure, there has not been a U.S. President in at least 20 years who has devoted more than a few hours to immersion in the issues of nuclear war doctrine—as opposed to independent decisions on weapons and arms control limitations—for reasons that will become apparent as you read on.

So What Is This Nuclear War "Doctrine" Business?

Perhaps the best way to approach the What-is-this-nuclear-war-doctrine-business question is to examine the simplest doctrine issue. Can a nuclear war be won? By win, we mean a win where both sides and the rest of the world agree, like when the U.S., the Soviet Union and the Allies won World War II.

Nothing is more disheartening to the newcomer to the debate over nuclear war doctrine than the awful realization that there is no consensus among experts in this country on what seems the most important of all questions: Do the leaders of the Soviet Union think they can "win" a nuclear war? Here is a question that, if answerable, would be crucial to a multitude of questions of U.S. defense posture and capability. But what's the answer? Is there an answer?

This chapter attempts to set out as simply and clearly as possible the debate around the question of strategic nuclear policy. The framework is that of "strategic doctrine," as it is known in the defense establishment, a phrase that is defined as:

> . . . a set of operative beliefs, values, and assertions that in a significant way guide official behavior with regard to strategic research and development (R&D), weapons choice, forces, operational plans, arms control, etc. The essence of U.S. "doctrine" is to deter central nuclear war at relatively low levels of arms effort through the credible threat of catastrophic damage to the enemy should deterence fail.[1]

---

[1]Fritz W. Ermarth, "Contrasts in American and Soviet Strategic Thought," *International Security* 3 (Fall 1978): 139-139.

As pointed out in the Introduction, there is absolutely no consensus in the United States as to U.S. "strategic doctrine." Furthermore, there is not a single official U.S. government document that contains "a set of operative beliefs, values, and assertions that *in a significant way* [emphasis added] guides official behavior with regard to strategic research and development (R&D), weapons choice, forces, operational plans, arms control, etc."

To be sure, there are occasional government-wide attempts to obtain such a document. But invariably by the time the process is finished, the Presidentially-approved documents (which have names like National Security Decision Memorandum 242, Presidential Directive 59) provide little direct guidance to "official behavior" in the areas cited above. For example, you would think that there would be a Presidentially approved document that says something like: "I would like U.S. second-strike retaliatory capability against the Soviet Union to be destruction of at least 70 percent of Soviet industrial capacity, 50 percent of the Soviet population, 90 percent of Soviet airfields, 90 percent of still-occupied Soviet ICBM silos, etc.," or "I believe the U.S. can accept bilateral reductions in nuclear force levels to 15,000 nuclear weapons and 1,200 intercontinental missiles and bombers on each side." But no such documents exist.

How then, you might ask, is "official behavior" in areas like weapons acquisition, weapons employment and arms control guided? Answer: the bureaucracy "wings it," makes it up as they go along. In fact, such basic questions rarely come up save in the occasional efforts (usually once per Presidential administration) to bridge this gap.

In light of the vagueness, disagreements and lack of operational significance of U.S. nuclear war doctrine, it should not be surprising to find that a discussion of Soviet doctrine makes for pretty thin gruel. Nevertheless, there are noteworthy similarities and differences in some of the "currents" that run through U.S. and Soviet pronouncements on such matters. Identifying those similarities and differences is at the heart of the debate around the nuclear doctrine issue. So sit back and learn—and don't be surprised if you sometimes feel you've gone through a time warp and are in a 16th-century ecclesiastical discussion.

The Name of the Game: Strategic Doctrine

There are five central issues that define the differences and similarities in U.S. and Soviet "strategic doctrine": (1) the phenomenon of deterrence—what it takes to stop the other side from attacking you; (2) the consequences of an all-out strategic nuclear war (the essence of the question of whether the Soviet leaders think they can "win" a nuclear war in some meaningful sense); (3) strategic conflict limitation—how the two sides view the idea of "limited nuclear war," however that might be defined; (4) stability—the minimization of incentives to acquire more nuclear weapons and to use them; and (5) distinctions and relationships between intercontinental and regional strategic security concerns—best exemplified by how forces in Europe relate to the U.S.-Soviet relationship.[2] (6) counterforce (targeting enemy strategic forces) vs. countervalue (targeting enemy population and industrial centers); (7) attitude toward a first strike (preemption); and (8) defense against nuclear attack—whether it is possible or not.[3]

The following pages contrast U.S. and Soviet views of these "strategic doctrine" and nuclear war issues.

The Concept of Deterrence

To date, there has been a rough symmetry between U.S. and Soviet views of deterrence: each side seeks to restrain the other through the threat of punitive action, up to and including destruction of the society through all-out war. But as one American Sovietologist, Robert Legvold, has observed, there is a critical difference in the *conception* of deterrence that each side embraces. According to Legvold:

For the United States, deterrence is an explicit intellectual construct, invented by civilians, and rooted in psychological or game theory, not the organizational theory of military science. For the Soviet Union, it is a residual concept, an effect produced by performing other military tasks well, tasks involving a deft foreign

---

[2]Ibid., p. 143.

[3]Richard Pipes, "Why the Soviet Union Thinks It Could Fight and Win a Nuclear War," *Commentary*, July 1977, p. 28.

policy and a carefully prepared defense. It is inexplicit, it has no texts, it even lacks an adequate name in Russian, and it is without authors, only overseers, and these are military leaders whose first concern is with success in war.[4]

Legvold goes on to explain how this essential difference in conception leads the U.S. to view deterrence in the context of "bargaining," focused more on the period before a war might occur than on war itself. By contrast, the Soviet Union focuses its attention on its war-fighting capability and in particular on "assured retaliatory capability," as another American expert in Soviet military policy, Raymond Garthoff, has called it.[5] But the Soviet Union also has a broader concept of deterrence in that it is seen as a means of protecting Soviet foreign policy in action, and what they perceive to be the favorable movement of the "correlation of forces" on a worldwide basis.

Independent of these differences, it is clear that both sides view the possession of a second strike (or retaliatory) "assured destruction" capability against the society of the other not only as a necessary condition for deterrence but in fact as the foundation stone for their nuclear policy. It takes a retaliatory force of roughly 1,000 nuclear weapons[6] to achieve this capability. The possession of this capability by both sides goes under the name "Mutual Assured Destruction" or MAD. (Mutual Assured Death would be a more appropriate term—the acronym can even be retained.)

Since only about 1,000 nuclear weapons are needed for MAD and each side possesses roughly 25,000 such weapons, much of the nuclear doctrine debate centers around why you need more—or why you think the other guy thinks he needs more.

---

[4] Robert Legvold, "Strategic 'Doctrine' and SALT: Soviet and American Views," *Survival*, Vol. XXI, no. 1 (January/February, 1979), p. 8.

[5] Raymond L. Garthoff, "Mutual Deterrence and Strategic Arms Limitation in Soviet Policy," *International Security* 3 (Summer 1978): 124.

[6] For both sides, 1,000 retaliating nuclear weapons is adequate to destroy every city down to a population of about 15,000 to 20,000 people.

Winning a Nuclear War

It has been an article of faith of U.S. political leaders and strategic planners for many years that a nuclear war is essentially "unwinnable," however winning might be defined in a realistic sense of the word. Obviously, it is hard to conceive of any U.S. political leader declaring that "We won!" if a nuclear war resulted in the destruction of any significant number of cities. (In fact, a senior White House official in a prior administration once remarked that a retaliatory attack of "one nuclear weapon on Washington, D.C., during working hours" would be sufficient to deter any U.S. President from attacking the Soviet Union.) For a time, at least, it appeared that Soviet leaders shared the view that nuclear war was "unwinnable."

In actual fact, a substantial debate on the issue took place in the Soviet Union during the Khrushchev era. The outcome of the debate, at least from the perspective of the outside observer, appears to have been ambiguous. First, it appears that, in the view of Fritz Ermarth:

> . . . the system decided it *had* to believe in survival and victory of some form. Not so to believe would mean that the most basic processes of history, on which Soviet ideology and political legitimacy are founded, could be derailed by the technological works of man and the caprice of an historically-doomed opponent. Moreover, as the defenders of doctrinal rectitude continued to point out, failure to believe in the "manageability" of nuclear disaster would lead to pacifism, defeatism, and lassitude in the Soviet military effort.[7]

In recent years, as Soviet military strength vis-à-vis the U.S. has grown, there are occasional expressions in the Soviet Union (as there occasionally are in the U.S.) that a nuclear war could be "won," in the sense that the Soviet Union would "survive" better than the U.S. On both sides, the possibility that the other side could win and the home country lose is also entertained.

The assessment of a Soviet perspective on "winning" a nuclear war that differs from that in the U.S. is, however, inconsistent with the recent (and frequent) public and propa-

---

[7]Ermarth, "Contrasts in American and Soviet Strategic Thought," p. 144.

ganda statements of Soviet political and military leaders. For example, in his address to the 26th Party Congress in February 1981, Brezhnev noted:

> The danger of war does indeed hang over the U.S. as it does over all countries in the world. But its source is not the Soviet Union, not its mythical superiority, but the arms race itself and the continuing tension in the world. We are prepared to combat this genuine, not imaginary, danger—hand in hand with America, with the European states, with all countries on our planet. *To try to prevail over the other side in the arms race or to count on victory in a nuclear war is dangerous madness.*

In sum, there remains some uncertainty as to whether Soviet perspectives on the winnability of a nuclear war differ in any significant way from those of U.S. leaders. Is it possible that a perceived ideological imperative has evolved in some meaningful way into a substantial belief in a strategic possibility of "winning" among those individuals in the Kremlin who will ultimately make the decision as to how, why and if the Soviet Union will choose to fight a nuclear war? It seems unlikely. It is hard to conceive of any leader (in the unlikely event he or she survives) declaring victory amidst the rubble of his or her cities as the struggle for survival in the postwar world begins. But we would certainly like to see them stop using the term "win" altogether.

They probably think the same thing about us.

The Idea of "Limited" Nuclear War

U.S. political and military decision-makers are divided on the question of whether a "limited" nuclear war is possible and whether strategic options should be developed that assume the capacity to limit nuclear war if and when deterrence fails. The first question focuses on psychological factors involving whether a national leader, or whoever might be in that position after the outbreak of a nuclear war, will be able to *resist* pressures to launch successively larger strikes against enemy targets. In fact, in the past, both sides have promised "massive retaliation"—and quickly.

While not well known, in the early 1960s U.S. strategists introduced the *concept* of limited nuclear war, in particular with respect to the possibility of a Soviet conventional attack on Western Europe. We declared that we would reserve judgment as to whether we would respond to such a Soviet conventional attack with massive nuclear retaliation or more limited use of "theater" or "battlefield" nuclear weapons.

The Soviet Union has been quick to denounce any suggestion that nuclear war could be limited in any manner, whether it be limited to a particular geographic region or to a small number of nuclear weapons launched by either side. Their objective, which many U.S. observers believe stems from a desire to fuel the U.S. debate on limited war policy, focuses on the same concern as U.S. critics: talking about a "limited" nuclear war makes the use of nuclear weapons more tolerable and thereby detracts from the effectiveness of the policy of deterrence. Some Europeans have joined the debate with charges that when the U.S. talks about limited nuclear war, they mean limited to Europe. An offhand remark in 1981 by President Reagan on confining a nuclear war to Europe further fueled this European concern.

It is noteworthy that very few national security experts in the United States believe that a nuclear war can be limited. While it is recognized that a limited nuclear war "does not violate any laws of physics," most individuals familiar with the shortcomings in the communications systems and other critical links believe it to be a practical impossibility. For example, Former Secretary of Defense Harold Brown has been quite explicit and outspoken on this question.

Stability in the Acquisition and Use of Nuclear Weapons

The concept of "stability" is frequently seen in U.S. discourses on the issue of nuclear war doctrine—but almost entirely absent in Soviet perspectives. U.S. thinking about "stability" emphasizes the desirability of reducing to the lowest level possible the incentives to acquire and to use nuclear weapons. This perspective underlies strong U.S. desires to negotiate "contracts" with the Soviet Union (for example, bilateral arms control agreements) in which a measure of "stability" is guaranteed by high-confidence projections of "mutual assured destruction," i.e., that our respective societies would assuredly be destroyed in the event of nuclear war (because our respective offensive forces could withstand attack and retaliate). This perspective was also manifest in a U.S. decision in the early 1970s not to build ICBMs capable of attacking and destroying Soviet fixed silo-based ICBMs. This decision, promulgated in correspondence between Senator Edmund Brooke and President Nixon and Secretary of Defense Melvin Laird, eschewed the building of ICBMs with so-called "counterforce" capability.

By contrast, the Soviet Union has been somewhat ambiguous in its view of stability, or at least what one can infer is its view of stability by its actions.

On the one hand, the Soviets did sign the ABM Treaty, limiting the deployment on both sides of this potentially "destabilizing" system, i.e., large ABM systems on both sides would have introduced significant uncertainty in "mutual assured destruction." On the other hand, Soviet acceptance of the ABM Treaty may well have been a reflection of their assessment of a significant U.S. lead in ABM technology. Soviet acceptance of the ABM Treaty has not prevented their continued research and development efforts on ABM technology, however, nor has it deterred comparable U.S. efforts.

Perhaps the most disturbing aspect of the Soviet view of stability is manifest in their decision to build and deploy a force of highly accurate SS-18 and SS-19 missiles capable of destroying with a high degree of confidence 80 to 90 percent of U.S. land-based ICBMs. In the U.S. view, this decision (and these weapon systems) are destabilizing—and especially galling because, as cited above, we passed up the opportunity to build and deploy such systems in the early 1970s.

On the other hand, we have recently doubled the yield (170 kilotons to 350 kilotons) and improved the accuracy of our 550 Minuteman III MIRVed ICBMs. At three warheads apiece, this force has a total of 1,650 "counterforce" warheads capable of destroying 70 to 80 percent of the 800 Soviet *MIRVed* ICBM force. Is this also destabilizing? That is one of the tough questions (see "counterforce" vs. "countervalue" discussion below) in the "stability" part of nuclear war doctrine.

Another perspective on the "stability" issue is found in the Soviet claim that U.S. deployment of Pershing II ballistic missiles and Tomahawk cruise missiles in Europe would be "destabilizing." The Pershing II has the capability to deliver nuclear warheads from West Germany to the Western USSR in less than eight minutes. Missiles from U.S. submarines in the Norwegian Sea can do the same thing in ten to twelve minutes. Does that difference make Pershing II destabilizing and U.S. submarine-launched ballistic missiles (SLBMs) not so? Or is it the fact that the Pershing II and the cruise missiles are based on the territory of U.S. allies that makes them destabilizing? If so, what's the logic?

A final perspective on stability is obtained from the U.S. and Soviet concern about the survivability of missile-carrying submarines. Given the U.S. anti-submarine warfare (ASW) capability, there is a much greater U.S. threat to Soviet submarines than vice versa. Is this destabilizing and should we restrain our ASW capability? If so, how do we deal with the need for ASW improvements for the conventional war "protect the convoys/sink his ships" mission?

As you can see, "stability," like beauty, is very much in the eye of the beholder. Nonetheless, you can expect each side to continue to speak of destabilizing moves by the other that could "spiral" into a new arms race, increase the risk of war and so forth.

The Relationship Between Intercontinental and Regional Security Concerns

When the U.S. and the Soviet Union agreed in the late 1960s to begin efforts to control the nuclear arms race, they decided to focus initially on "strategic" nuclear weapons. But when they actually sat down at the negotiating table, it became apparent that the two sides had differing concepts of "strategic" and "nonstrategic" forces. They agreed that ICBMs, intercontinental bombers and submarine-launched missiles were "strategic." But the Soviet Union had a longer list, seeking to include within the definition of strategic forces intermediate-range weapons (missiles and bombers), which we consider part of the "theater" forces that constitute "forward defense" in places such as Western Europe. Their argument was that these weapons could reach Soviet territory—and were therefore "strategic". In turn they argued that comparable missiles and bombers on their side should be kept out of the negotiations on the grounds that they couldn't reach the United States.

The Soviets first strongly resisted, and then grudgingly accepted, the segregation of what the U.S. calls "forward-based systems"—NATO nuclear weapons deployed in Europe and on aircraft carriers in the European theater—from the U.S.-Soviet strategic arms limitations talks (SALT I and II). At the same time, the Soviets have continued to argue that all U.S. *and* NATO nuclear forces capable of reaching Soviet territory are part of the West's "strategic" arsenal. This more comprehensive Soviet view has been reinforced in recent years by the emergence of China as a hostile power on its eastern borders.

The planned U.S. deployment in Europe of Pershing II ballistic missiles and Tomahawk ground-launched missiles has further aroused Soviet concern about the role of U.S. "forward-based systems." While the rationale for these missiles is the need for a NATO response to the Soviet deployment of SS-20 IRBMs, the Soviets see these systems as one more example of the U.S. taking advantage of their European alliance to place nuclear weapons closer to Soviet territory.

"Counterforce" vs. "Countervalue" Targeting

The U.S. concept of deterrence gives major emphasis to "countervalue" targeting—the holding of enemy population and industrial centers hostage as a deterrent to an enemy "first strike" attack. The underlying assumption is that the threat of the almost total destruction of the Soviet industrial capacity and the immediate death of some 120 million Soviet citizens is more than sufficient to keep a Soviet finger off the button. In particular, supporters of this view point to the enormous destruction and loss of life in the Soviet Union in World War II to emphasize the point that, far better than we in the U.S., Soviet leaders know the horror of war.

Ironically, the detractors of this viewpoint stress that Soviet leaders are far less interested in protection of their citizens and industry than in protecting their own nuclear deterrent and point to this same World War II experience as proof that Soviet leaders have shown themselves willing to take appalling losses to achieve political and military objectives. As a consequence, they argue that Soviet targeting is primarily oriented toward a "counterforce" strategy—the targeting of enemy nuclear forces—thereby undermining not so much the will but the capacity of the enemy to retaliate.

In the "real" world of nuclear targeting, the distinction between an emphasis on "counterforce" versus "countervalue" targeting is largely irrelevant, since both sides possess adequate nuclear forces to do both. Each side possesses the capability to deliver roughly 10,000 nuclear weapons to the other's territory in a first strike, roughly 5,000 in a second strike. As noted above, since it only takes 1,000 nuclear weapons to destroy every city in the U.S. or the Soviet Union with a population over 15 to 20,000 people, this leaves an awesome capability to attack "counterforce" targets—at least those which are vulnerable. In this context, U.S. ICBM forces are today more vulnerable than the Soviet's (see above discussion). U.S. deployment of the M-X, ICBM or Trident II submarine-launched missile would change that. In contrast, Soviet submarine and bomber forces are far more vulnerable than U.S. forces, a situation that is unlikely to change for the foreseeable future.

Preemptive Strike: The Bolt from the Blue

Both the Soviet Union, with the German invasion in the summer of 1941, and the United States, with the Japanese attack on Pearl Harbor six months later, were victims of surprise attacks at the start of World War II. For the U.S., the consequence was the near loss of our Pacific fleet; for the Soviet Union, the consequence was the near loss of the entire country.

The impact of this experience on the two countries has varied. Because nuclear weapons can be delivered in a matter of minutes and their destruction potential is so great, there is an acknowledged premium on launching a preemptive first strike against an enemy's strategic forces, if one's objective is to minimize his capacity to respond, or against his cities and industry, if one's objective is to minimize his will to respond. Some analysts in the U.S. believe that the Soviet Union would never launch a preemptive first strike against U.S. strategic forces because it could never succeed in "preempting" our retaliatory capability—we would always have our submarine-based weapons, a major portion of our bomber forces and at least a fraction of our land-based forces (assuming that none of our ICBMs were "launched on warning").

The detractors from this position argue that Soviet offensive doctrine and its own World War II experience have ingrained in the minds of Soviet political and military leaders the value of launching a preemptive first strike against the enemy, even knowing the risks and possible consequences, should an enemy attack appear imminent.

At this time, U.S. policy stresses that for ICBMs and submarines it will not "launch on warning" of an enemy attack, but will launch bombers on such warning because they can be recalled. Surviving forces would then respond, with the promised response being a massive strike against Soviet population and industrial centers and Soviet military targets. At the same time, there is some interest in adopting "launch under attack" posture for ICBMs in which missiles would be launched once there is unambiguous information (e.g., warning plus nuclear detonation) that an attack is taking place. At present such a policy would not save many additional ICBMs, but there are several M-X basing plans (including "Dense Pack") that would make such a policy potentially feasible.

As far as the Soviet Union is concerned, we are not certain what their policy is with regard to "launch on warning." We hope that it is the same as ours. The known instances where our warning system has erroneously signaled a Soviet attack against the U.S. have reinforced our commitment to this policy, and we assume that our experience has probably been mirrored in the Soviet Union.

In Conclusion . . . The Hope (or Hopelessness) of Defense Against a Nuclear Attack

U.S. concepts of strategic deterrence argue that there can be only a very limited defense against nuclear attack—that ABM defenses cannot reliably stop incoming missiles, air defenses cannot reliably stop incoming airplanes, and that once nuclear weapons are detonated, there is little anyone can do to protect people and facilities. Further, U.S. strategists argue that such measures, in that they imply an effort to survive a nuclear strike, threaten the delicate "balance of terror" on which mutual deterrence depends.

In recent years, the U.S. has moved somewhat away from its earlier strong adherence to this position and now spends about $100 million annually for a variety of civil defense measures, with a concentration on planning for crisis evacuation and relocation of the population for all major metropolitan areas. But we have not changed our position on air defenses. Today, there are only a few squadrons of U.S. fighter aircraft deployed for air defense, and they could do little more than protect us against an air attack by a country like Cuba.

In the case of ABM, both the U.S. and the Soviet Union are prohibited from any significant deployment of ABM systems by the 1972 SALT I ABM Treaty. This treaty recently completed the second of its five-year reviews with neither side proposing changes in the treaty.

The Soviet Union has traditionally shown somewhat more interest in defense against nuclear attack. The Soviets have a nationwide civil defense program under military control with an estimated annual budget of $2 billion. The two objectives of the program are (1) like the U.S., crisis evacuation and relocation planning, and (2) the survival, not of the entire population and physical facilities but of the political leadership, from the national government down to the local level, and, to a lesser extent, critical factory workers. Pentagon estimates put the number of government and Party officials targeted for protection at approximately 110,000.

There is considerable debate about the potential effectiveness of the Soviet civil defense system. For example, the plan for evacuating Moscow calls for most of the population to walk out of the city, since there is inadequate motorized transport to move 8 million people. This would take three to seven days, would be enormously difficult in the severe Soviet winter months and would almost certainly spark a matching U.S. evacuation effort. The shelter system is also suspect for all the reasons shelters have been suspect before—susceptibility to destruction by blast, fire, heat and oxygen deprivation because of their proximity to factories and cities targeted by the U.S. countervalue strategy.[8]

8For more detail, see Ground Zero, *Nuclear War: What's in It for You?* (New York: Pocket Books, 1982), chap. 5.

In summarizing Soviet civil defense efforts, the recent Pentagon study, *Soviet Military Power,* emphasized:

> A civil defense problem of vital concern to the Soviets is their continuing inability to provide physical protection for their industrial installations. Although there have been numerous references in Soviet civil defense literature to the desirability of the dispersal of key industries for protection purposes, little has been done to achieve this goal.

Chapter 19

If Only It Were a Fable: The History of Arms Control in the Nuclear Age

This is the semisad tale of the United States, the Soviet Union and arms control in the nuclear age. It is principally the story of a U.S.-Soviet effort to control the buildup of *nuclear* arms—theirs, ours and others'—as a means for reducing the risk of nuclear war. It is not a success story.

At the same time it is not a story of failure—at least not yet. There have been some arms control agreements that can be characterized as "modest, but useful" (the Joint Chiefs of Staff description of the SALT II Treaty) and the effort is still continuing. And, in fact, arms control may someday be part of a larger success story—the tale of how the human community, led by the nuclear superpowers, found a path away from nuclear war. But so far it is largely a tale of frustration and dashed hopes. A U.S. arms control negotiator once remarked, "You don't make arms control agreements with your friends." He might have added, ". . . and you don't make many arms control agreements with your enemies, either."

Like any history, the story that follows has the benefit of hindsight—the "Couldn't they see what they were doing (or not doing)?" sort of perspective of the Monday morning quarterback. Sometimes that's not fair. But this is probably not one of those cases. The impact of "unleashing the power of the atom," as Einstein put it, the need he saw to change our "modes of thinking," was clear from the time that the first atomic bomb exploded in the desert of Alamogordo, New Mexico. The atomic scientists recognized this immediately and tried to shake the world into realizing what they had discovered—and what they had done. But hardly anyone listened. Governments aren't very good at foresight.

The Baruch Plan: Have I Got a Deal for You

In the period immediately after World War II, the case for controlling nuclear weapons (or atomic bombs, as they were then called) was sufficiently strong that President Truman called for a study commission to recommend a policy for dealing with these weapons. The effort was chaired by Secretary of State Dean Acheson and David Lilienthal, who later headed up the first Atomic Energy Commission. Their report recommended that nuclear weapons be placed under some kind of international control. The proposed plan, called the Baruch Plan (after New York financier Bernard Baruch, who presented the recommendations to the UN), called for establishing an international body to control all existing nuclear weapons and the means of production. But there was a hooker in the offer: until such time as the international body was established and functioning, the U.S. would (1) keep control of all of its nuclear weapons, and (2) continue to test and produce nuclear weapons.

Baruch argued at the UN that the U.S. proposal was a generous step by the United States, in light of our nuclear monopoly. The Soviets generously told us to forget it, proposing instead a meaningless plan under which the U.S. would first destroy all of its nuclear weapons.

Why did the Soviets not pick up on the U.S. offer? Probably for lots of reasons having to do with both trust and competition. They were well on their way to their own nuclear bomb. Their atomic scientists knew they could do it and so did ours. The biggest secret of nuclear weapons—that they work—was already out. And, after all, you didn't expect a nation that claimed superiority in government, economy, and people, and the invention of everything from soup to nuts, to accept a brand of technological inferiority to the other claimant to the status of Number One. Just imagine an American-Russian conversation in 1945 over whose country was most responsible for the defeat of Hitler and the Third Reich.

And then there was the question of trust. The Russians didn't trust us. They didn't believe that our offer to place nuclear weapons under international control was serious.

Perhaps they didn't believe that a nation with a monopoly on such an awesome weapon would give it up and that we were just trying to restrict their efforts to build nuclear weapons. If we were serious, why weren't we immediately suspending production and testing of nuclear weapons—a freeze, in current parlance? They undoubtedly focused on the fact that we were the only ones who had ever tested or built nuclear weapons. Thus, any negotiated constraint on nuclear weapons testing and production would give us a tremendous advantage for "breakout" in the event future events led to failure of the international body.

Were we really serious? It's not clear. The Baruch plan did not have the full support of all parts of the U.S. government. The military was particularly skeptical, especially about the verification problem, and it was never clear whether a forthcoming Soviet response could have led to an agreement on international control.

The Bear, the Bison and a Small First Effort

After the collapse of the Baruch Plan, the Russians went ahead and built their atomic bomb (first exploded in 1949). Then we both built hydrogen bombs. Then we surrounded the Soviet Union with B-47 bombers with nukes. Then they built the Bear and Bison intercontinental bombers, revealed them to us in the 1954 and 1955 May Day parades, and nuclear war came home to the United States.

That was not an easy time for the United States—or the Soviet Union. It was the height of the Cold War, and both nations were acutely aware of how easily the Cold War could become a hot war. So we made a little, tiny, microscopic effort to make friends (remember those pictures of Nikita Khrushchev with farmers in Iowa?) and also a little, tiny, microscopic effort to get a handle on what clearly was about to become the greatest arms race of all time by entering a moratorium on nuclear weapons testing.

A moratorium means maybe you're serious, maybe you're not. Neither side is sure because, of course, neither one trusts the other as far as he can kick him. So the Soviets shot down our U-2, Khrushchev banged his shoe at the UN, and in 1961, the Soviets broke the moratorium on some flimsy excuse. The total elapsed time of the moratorium was a little over twenty months.

The series of tests that followed on both sides was notable in that it included a Soviet test of the largest nuclear explosion that we know of—50 million tons of TNT in explosive power. Now, what does a 50-megaton bomb mean to you? It's hard to get a handle on, but someone calculated that a 50-megaton bomb would set fire to the entire state of Connecticut.

Then in 1962, we had the Cuban missile crisis. "We were eyeball-to-eyeball, and I think the other guy just blinked," said then Secretary of State Dean Rusk. "You'll never do that to us again," said the Soviet Deputy Foreign Minister, Valery Kuznetsov.

There was a clear lesson from this period and the first failed effort at arms control: negotiating arms control agreements in the nuclear age was not going to be easy, and the fortunes of arms control would be affected by the U.S.-Soviet relationship.

Let's Try Again

Sobered by the Cuban missile crisis and a growing public concern about nuclear weapons testing in the atmosphere, the United States and the Soviet Union decided in 1963 to try to negotiate a treaty limiting nuclear weapons testing. In September 1963, Ambassador Averell Harriman flew to Moscow as head of the U.S. negotiating team. In the late 1950s, the U.S. had sought a Comprehensive Test Ban—a CTB, as the experts frequently call it. At that point in time, both sides had conducted hundreds of nuclear weapons tests and there were sound arguments for stopping testing altogether—as well as some arguments against such a far-reaching proposal. In the latter category there were military concerns that without testing, confidence in the reliability of existing weapons would erode if *all* tests were halted.

In the early negotiations, CTB efforts failed on a simple point of verification with respect to the testing of nuclear weapons. We insisted on eight monitoring stations in the Soviet Union; they would only agree to three. The two did agree, however, to a Limited Test Ban Treaty (LTBT) prohibiting nuclear weapons testing in the atmosphere, in the oceans and in space. Nuclear weapons testing would move underground. We were confident about our ability to detect nuclear weapons tests in the atmosphere, oceans and space, but not about tests underground. The chief means of detecting underground nuclear weapons tests are seismic stations, which are otherwise used for detecting earthquakes. And therein lay the problem. Small underground nuclear weapons tests look just like earthquakes to seismic stations.

So we settled for an "LTBT" instead of a "CTB." It was the first arms control treaty of the nuclear age. As a means of limiting the environmental impact of nuclear weapons testing in the atmosphere, it was a profound success. As a means of controlling the U.S.-Soviet arms race, it was a failure. Nuclear weapons testing simply moved underground.

Nevertheless, the LTBT was an important first step. It showed the superpowers that they could successfully negotiate treaties in the nuclear realm. And it ushered in a period of great hope for arms control. In fact, it could be said that it marked the end of an era in which both we and the Soviets sought security in the nuclear age exclusively from weapons and began seeking security from weapons *and* arms control.

Arms Control Objectives: Whose Music Do We Dance To?

Within a few years of the Cuban missile crisis, the growing Soviet strategic capability and the issue of nuclear proliferation substantially depreciated the idea that building more and better weapons was a route to greater security, and we in the United States turned seriously to the pursuit of arms control. Our objectives were:

1. To limit the avenues or realms of US-Soviet nuclear competition;
2. To prevent the Soviets from surpassing us in weapons;
3. To restrict the spread of nuclear weapons to other countries;
4. Eventually to move away from the mutual reign of terror—the "mutual assured destruction" of the nuclear standoff.

At the same time, we really were not sure what Soviet objectives would be in entering serious arms control negotiations. We were encouraged by their willingness to agree to a limited test ban treaty, but, as noted above, that treaty did not in any serious way slow the nuclear arms race. We assumed that Soviet arms control objectives mirrored ours, but, of course, always ascribed to them the additional objective of trying to obtain military advantage through arms control negotiations. Undoubtedly somewhere in the Kremlin there is a memo that says that the Soviet Union should be suspicious of the United States in arms control negotiations for the same reason.

A Breathing Space in Outer Space

By the mid-1960s it was clear that arms control would be a major focus of US-Soviet efforts to control the arms race and reduce the risk of nuclear war. The first effort of significance was the outer space treaty. This treaty, negotiated under UN auspices in 1967, prohibited nuclear weapons and other weapons of "mass destruction" in outer space. At the time, neither we nor the Soviets could see a particular advantage to expanding the vigorous competition in nuclear armed missiles and bombers to the space environment. This situation is, of course, in sharp contrast to that which prevails today, where there is increasing talk of space being the new arena for competition.

The outer space treaty dramatically restricts the opportunities for space competition, especially when combined with the SALT I Anti-Ballistic Missile Treaty described below. The ability of the United States and the Soviet Union and other countries of the world to agree to keep space free from military competition points up the foresight that prevailed at the time this treaty was negotiated. In fact, by negotiating space as a sanctuary from military competition, our hope is that a significant barrier to such a competition has now been created: whoever wishes to open up this new arena must abrogate the treaty or withdraw from it and suffer the challenges of the international community as a whole.

The outer space treaty also exemplifies another of the fundamental lessons we have learned in arms control—that it is far easier to agree not to do something one has not done than it is to undo what has already been done.

The next major arms control accomplishment was the Nonproliferation Treaty of 1968. In this treaty, the "have" nuclear weapons states talked the "have not" states (or almost all of them) into agreeing not to try to get nuclear weapons. However, it is increasingly dubious whether this treaty can, in the long run, meet its objective of halting the spread of nuclear weapons. Several key nations have refused to sign the treaty, including two (China and France) that have significant nuclear arsenals and two (India and Israel) that appear to have developed nuclear weapons capability. Nonetheless, the NPT has probably slowed the spread of nuclear weapons, a significant contribution. When it comes to nuclear weapons, we need all the time we can get. If there are to be more nuclear weapons states, then, as one observer recently put it, "Less is better, later is better and farther away is better."

The nuclear club nations talked the non-nuclear nations into signing up for the NPT by promising two things: (1) that the non-nuclear weapons states would be supplied with the technology for nuclear power if they would not develop nuclear weapons, and, simultaneously, (2) the nuclear weapons states would negotiate toward nuclear arms limitations. However, since then it has become increasingly clear that it is relatively easy to legally or illegally reprocess the fuel from a nuclear reactor to extract the fissionable material that is used to make nuclear weapons. As a consequence, the nuclear weapons states (and some of the other nations that have developed nuclear power) have become increasingly concerned about supplying nuclear power to non-nuclear weapons states. Moreover, the superpowers and the other nuclear weapons states have never really honored the "promise" that they would slow down the buildup in nuclear arms. For that reason, at the most recent Nonproliferation Review Conference in 1980, the U.S. and USSR came under severe criticism from non-nuclear nations for not doing more to limit their own weapons production programs.

The Soviet Union probably deserves a better grade than any of the nuclear weapons states in terms of supplying nuclear reactors that could be used in the production of nuclear weapons. If everyone were getting a grade on this, the U.S. would probably get a B +, the Soviet Union would get an A and countries like France, Germany and Switzerland would get a D. If the proliferation of nuclear weapons continues, it will be these latter three countries that will be principally responsible, both in terms of their aggressive selling of reactors and in terms of not being as demanding in their inspection requirements as is probably needed to insure the control of the spread of nuclear weapons.

Salt I—A Winner for Both Sides

The next major agreement in the nuclear realm was SALT I. This agreement had two parts to it. The first, and by far the most important part, was the Anti-Ballistic Missile Treaty. In fact, this treaty is probably without question the paramount accomplishment of arms control to date. Under the terms of this treaty, the United States and the Soviet Union agreed to forego the building of significant antiballistic missile systems. Each side is permitted the deployment of a single ABM system to defend either one city or one missile site. As a consequence, both nations have effectively agreed to be in a state of vulnerability to missile attack. This vulnerability makes a major contribution to insuring the predictability of the outcome of a nuclear war.

The other half of the SALT I agreement was the so-called Interim Agreement on offensive weapons. This agreement was the culmination of over two and one-half years of attempts to negotiate a comprehensive agreement on offensive weapons. Against that objective, it was a failure. However, it did begin the process of limiting these weapons, and in the course of the SALT I negotiations on offensive systems, many of the critical issues that were to plague strategic nuclear arms control in the 1970s were highlighted.

Foremost among these issues was the question of which systems were to be included. Less than a year after the start of the SALT negotiations in August of 1970, the United States put forth a comprehensive proposal to limit ICBMs, submarine-launched ballistic missiles and bombers to a level of 1,900 systems. This proposal was rejected by the Soviets as a basis for negotiation for one primary reason: it did not include U.S. "forward-based aircraft." These were U.S. aircraft, F-4s and F-111s in Europe and A-6s and A-7s on carriers, that were within striking distance of the Soviet Union. Soviet insistence on including these systems highlighted two Soviet concerns: (1) "being surrounded" by hostile U.S. and NATO forces dating back to the late 1940s, and (2) U.S. forward-basing of nuclear systems gave it an advantage over the Soviet Union that should not be perpetuated through arms control.

A second problem highlighted in SALT I was that of the range of systems to be included in the arms control agreements. After some initial thoughts about including shorter-range cruise missiles and shorter-range ballistic missiles in Europe, the two sides settled on a framework that included ICBMs, submarine-launched ballistic missiles and so-called "heavy" bombers. In the end, however, as indicated above, they disagreed over whether forward-based systems should be included. As a consequence, the interim agreement covered only submarine-launched ballistic missiles and ICBMs, and in the current parlance could be characterized as a freeze on these systems. It froze the number of silo-based ICBMs on the two sides, and, to a degree, the number of launchers for submarine ballistic missiles. However, the Soviets were allowed to turn in roughly 200 older ICBMs and complete the building of some 200 submarine launchers, which they claimed were already in the process of construction.

The negotiations on the SALT I interim agreement also highlighted what has become in some way the biggest challenge to nuclear arms control; the forces the two sides have deployed and have in the pipeline are dramatically different in character.

Perhaps the greatest failure of SALT I was the inability to obtain limitations on multiple warhead systems (MIRVs). There was a substantial constituency in the United States to limit MIRVs, and in April 1970 the U.S. proposed a ban on the testing and deployment of MIRVs, conditional upon on-site inspection. Most analysts have questioned the seriousness of the U.S. MIRV ban proposal, not least because of its submission less than two months before Minuteman III deployment was scheduled to, and did in fact, begin. Some accounts even suggest that the wide-ranging, on-site inspection condition was added at the insistence of the Joint Chiefs of Staff mainly to insure that the proposal would be rejected by the USSR.

Predictably, the Soviet counterproposal, a MIRV production and deployment ban, the seriousness of which was also highly questionable, rejected the on-site inspection condition as well as the test ban on MIRVs themselves. The speed of the subsequent U.S. decision to drop the MIRV proposal (three months later) suggested lack of a deep commitment to the idea of restraining MIRV systems. It would have been an extraordinarily bold and ambitious move in the new realm of nuclear arms limitation, but it could not overcome the caution with which both sides were approaching this new effort at cooperation in solving military problems. Looking back on this period, Henry Kissinger later remarked, "I wish I had thought through more fully the implications of a MIRVed world."

SALT II—Final Exam of an Era

The SALT I agreement had been signed in Moscow in May of 1972 in a fanfare of celebration. It was to be the beginning of an era of peace and détente, and both President Nixon and President Brezhnev heralded the accomplishments of SALT I and highlighted their hopes for the future. In October of 1972, the SALT I agreements had been overwhelmingly approved by the Congress—with the Senate vote for both being 88 to 2.

Unfortunately, the 1972 signing and ratification of the SALT I agreements proved to be the high point of both détente and U.S.-Soviet relations.

In the fall of 1972, SALT II negotiations began. Their objective was to replace the crude Interim Agreement by a comprehensive, long-term treaty limiting offensive strategic weapons. The opening positions of both the U.S. and the Soviet Union in SALT II were "sweetheart deals." Both defined as their opening positions agreements that would have given them profound advantages in the strategic competition. In addition, the negotiations were initially handicapped by the lack of high-level attention on both sides. As a consequence, negotiating a mutually acceptable set of limitations took nearly seven years.

The negotiations ran into two problems at the outset: (1) the question of what was to be included in the agreement; and (2) the verification problem. In the first category, the Soviets again raised the problem of forward-based systems, and the first two years of SALT II negotiations in Geneva were spent with the Soviets raising the forward-based system issue on an almost weekly basis.

But it was verification that was to prove the most challenging issue of SALT II.

Because the forces on the two sides were so different and because they had been developed in an environment that gave no thought to future arms control, the challenge of imposing limitations on the spectrum of offensive systems that prevailed at that time was extraordinary. In addition, it had been clear in the ratification proceedings for SALT I that much more stringent attention needed to be paid to verification. It would not be an exaggeration to say that of the seven years spent on SALT II, something like 80 to 85 percent of the effort was expended on negotiating appropriate verification limits—called "collateral constraints."

Another problem that plagued SALT II was the gradually increasing "weakness" of the governments on both sides during the critical early years of the negotiations. By the time it was realized that SALT II was going to require an extraordinary amount of high-level effort—which some would say should have been apparent from the beginning—the Nixon administration was deep into the Watergate scandal and there was little hope of either Nixon or Kissinger using his extraordinary stature to push through the kind of compromises that were needed on the U.S. side. Then in early 1976, President Ford pulled back from an imminent agreement in order not to have to defend that agreement against the conservative challenge of Ronald Reagan in the 1976 Presidential campaign. On the Soviet side, with Leonid Brezhnev in poor health and pressed by other concerns, the situation was not much better. Nevertheless, in the end, after nearly seven years of negotiations and the passage of the U.S. Presidency from Nixon to Ford to Carter, in June of 1979 the SALT II Treaty was signed. (The highlights of the treaty are described in Appendix 3.)

The treaty was initially greeted with skepticism, but after the first set of Congressional hearings in July of 1979, it seemed likely that the Joint Chiefs of Staff characterization of the treaty—"modest, but useful,"—would prevail. But then, in August of 1979, a Soviet combat brigade was identified in Cuba, raising a long-standing question regarding Soviet objectives in the Western Hemisphere, their trustworthiness and so on. The Carter administration was staggered by this development but gradually started putting its ratification effort together again in the fall of 1979. The taking of the U.S. hostages in Iran in November of 1979 again slowed the SALT II ratification process, which was now proceeding in an environment of much greater suspicion of the Soviets. That suspicion was further fanned when the Soviet Union invaded Afghanistan in late December of 1979. Shortly thereafter, President Carter asked the Senate to suspend consideration of the treaty.

With the Soviet invasion, SALT II went onto the back burner, where it is to this day. Curiously, however, as of early 1983, both sides were continuing to abide by its terms.

It is also interesting that the failure of SALT II may have been in the long-term interests of us all, because without that failure, it was unlikely that the current public interest in the nuclear war problem would have ever taken place.

TTBT and PNE: An Arms Control Way Station

In the spring of 1974, with preparations underway for a third Nixon-Brezhnev Summit in June and SALT II going nowhere, the arms control communities of both superpowers were challenged to come up with something to "showcase" at the summit. The result was two minor, but nevertheless interesting, agreements. The first of these, the Threshold Test Ban Treaty (TTBT) took a small step toward a Comprehensive Test Ban Treaty (CTBT) by limiting nuclear weapons tests to 150 kilotons. The second, the Treaty on Peaceful Nuclear Explosions (PNE) laid out strict ground rules for the testing and use of so-called "peaceful" nuclear explosions (for building canals, dams, etc.), an option neither side has much interest in anymore.

While neither Treaty has been ratified, both have been informally adhered to by both superpowers. As described in the next chapter, the major significance of these Treaties was the Soviet acceptance of a very limited form of on-site inspection.

A Small START for the Reagan Administration

When the Reagan administration took office in January of 1981, the Soviets sat back and waited for the expected shift in the U.S. nuclear arms control position they felt certain was coming. For the Soviets, such discontinuities are very difficult to accept; in fact, it drives them nuts. They knew some continuity under President Nixon and initially under President Ford. But even Ford shifted tracks on them in early 1976, departing from an agreement that in January of 1976 was within a few details of being settled to propose a dramatically different and new approach to the negotiations. Then when the Carter administration took office in January 1977, the Soviets hoped to pick up on the January 1976 position. Instead, they found themselves facing a wholly new proposal. Perhaps most galling was a U.S. proposal to throw out fifteen months of excruciating negotiations on cruise missile limitations and an agreed settlement on so-called "heavy" ICBMs. In private they often grumbled that they thought they were negotiating with "the United States of America" rather than being guests at a movable feast.

Thus, by the time the Reagan administration took office, the Soviets were not shocked (but probably no less galled) at a new approach to arms control. For starters, the Reagan approach manifested little interest in the subject, claiming instead that arms control had lulled the United States into ignoring the need for a build-up in nuclear forces. However, when it became clear that, for economic and technical reasons, the option of a big build-up in U.S. nuclear forces was not an option at all, and U.S. anti-nuclear protests argued for more attention to restraining the nuclear arms race and other nuclear war issues, the Reagan administration agreed to begin arms control negotiations, but with these shifts from the Carter administration arms control position:

(1) Negotiations would only take place in the areas of long-range (strategic) and intermediate range nuclear forces, thus putting off the negotiation on a Comprehensive Test Ban and a treaty limiting anti-satellite weapons.

(2) To emphasize a primary goal of reductions, the name of the new strategic forces negotiations would be START (Strategic Arms *Reduction* Talks) rather than SALT (Strategic Arms *Limitations* Talks).

The opening U.S. position in the START negotiations called not only for reductions—to an aggregate ICBM/SLBM long-range bomber level of 1,600—but also for a dramatic restructuring of Soviet forces. Simply put, the U.S. proposal, especially in a call for de-emphasizing and reducing Soviet ICBM forces to one-third their current size, called for the Soviet Union to restructure their forces along the lines of U.S. forces. In addition, the U.S. position called for limits on the production of long-range missiles with accompanying, but as yet unspecified, collateral constraints, *viz.*, onsite inspection, to insure adequate verification.

By contrast, the Soviet position called for, first, ratification of SALT II, and then a modest next-steps agreement with some reductions. However, the Soviets, not unexpectedly, did reopen the issues of U.S. forward-based systems and the nuclear systems of U.S. allies (Britain and France), arguing that these issues could not be pushed aside in the context of reduced force levels.

Obviously the two sides have begun the START negotiations from positions that are miles apart—in fact, there is no precedent in the history of strategic arms control for such a broad gap between the two sides. This obviously gives rise to several basic questions with respect to further progress in nuclear arms control. Is there any hope that an agreement on intermediate-range nuclear forces (see following section) can be completed without a parallel agreement on longer-range systems? Are the two sides really committed to more far-reaching nuclear arms control at this time? Or can they be so committed without a more fundamental change in the U.S.-Soviet relationship?

Intermediate-Range Nuclear Forces: If You Thought SALT/START Were Difficult . . .

In late 1979, with SALT II completed (but not ratified), the U.S. and its allies turned to the problem of limiting intermediate-range nuclear forces (INF). Facing a continuing buildup in the Soviet medium-range, three-warhead SS-20 mobile missile (2,500 mile range), the NATO allies decided to go forward with the deployment in Europe of 108 Pershing II ballistic missiles (1000 km range) and 464 Tomahawk ground-launched cruise missiles (1,500 mile range). In addition, an overture to the Soviets to begin negotiating limits on these intermediate-range forces was made—and accepted. Initial discussions took place late in the Carter administration and the negotiations began in earnest in the Reagan administration.

The initial Reagan proposal (the so-called "Zero Option") called for both sides to abandon altogether intermediate-range land-based missile systems—essentially an offer not to deploy the Pershing II and the Tomahawk cruise missiles if the Soviets tore down all of their 250-plus SS-20s and their nearly 400 older SS-4s and SS-5s.

The Soviets responded in late 1982 by offering to cut their SS-20 force to the level of the French and British intermediate-range missiles (currently a total of 160 missiles) if the U.S. did not go forward with the Pershing II and cruise missile deployments.

The sides are still far apart in these negotiations. They have not even settled on the number limits, much less face the lesson of SALT that "the devil is in the details." In particular, these intermediate-range missiles will present an extraordinary challenge to verification because of their size.

Anthrax and Arms Control:
Bad News on the Doorstep

While this chapter has focused on U.S.-Soviet arms control in the nuclear weapons arena, there is a lesson from another arms control realm, biological weapons, that is germane to both nuclear arms control and U.S.-Soviet relations.

In the spring of 1979, there was an acknowledged outbreak of anthrax in the Soviet city of Sverdlovsk. The available evidence seemed to indicate that this was not, as the Soviets claimed, an isolated incident of diseased meat but rather an incident involving an explosion at a production facility for the anthrax toxin. Since production of such toxins is a violation of the 1972 Biological Weapons Treaty, the U.S. called on the Soviets to clarify what had happened. In response, the Soviets have stuck with their original story and, unfortunately, the Biological Weapons Treaty contains no provisions for inspections or a more formal consultative forum (like the SALT Standing Consultative Commission) in which to take up such a situation.

There are lessons for all arms control negotiations in this impasse. The first is that any treaty written in vague language (as is the case here) makes it difficult to determine whether a violation has taken place. The second is that the absence of a formal consultative forum to deal with suspected violations severely hampers treaty implementation. Finally, however inadequate the Treaty language and procedures are, it is important for signatories to try and establish exactly what has happened in such ambiguous situations— which has certainly not been done in the Sverdlovsk case.

The Verdict on Arms Control

"The jury is still out" on arms control. Both we and the Soviets continue to believe that controlling our own arms competition—and the build-up of nuclear arms in other nations—is a *necessary* condition for finding our way out of the current morass. But is it *sufficient*—in the way the eggs are necessary if you want to bake a cake, but not sufficient to guarantee success? The historian Barbara Tuchman explored this question in a June 1982 article in the *New York Times Sunday Magazine*. She reviewed the arms control efforts of the past—from the pre-World War I naval agreements through the pre-World War II agreements—and observed that all exhibited modest, but useful accomplishments, but none prevented war. She points a finger at the leaders of the governments involved (carefully noting that they were *men*) and argues that they were not sufficiently committed to preventing war.

Will the story be different this time? Is the commitment to prevent nuclear war strong enough—so that the effort to control arms will someday be heralded as a critical ingredient in a success story without equal?

It will not be enough to claim someday that arms control *nearly* prevented World War III. That would be a story of failure. "Close" only counts in horseshoes.

Chapter 20

Trust Is Earned, Not Given: The Problem of Verification

An astute student of U.S.-Soviet affairs once observed that one of our problems in the United States was that we would rather be working the nuclear war problem with the Canadians. (And the Soviets would probably rather be working the problem with the Outer Mongolians). Unfortunately for both superpowers, there is no escaping the extraordinary challenge of working this problem with each other. And in no realm is this more striking than in the issue of verifying arms control limitations.

The verification problem has its roots in several pieces of "baggage" that both sides bring to the arms control arena. Among the most important of these is the extraordinary diversity in weapons systems and their characteristics: *not a single weapon system in existence today was designed with an eye to the verification problem.* As a consequence, every proposed arms control limitation requires careful examination of a family of weapon systems which may or may not be covered by the limitation, depending on fine points of definition. For example, U.S. and Soviet negotiators might agree in principle to limit submarine-launched cruise missiles. The next set of questions includes:

1. Will the limit be the same for nuclear and conventionally armed cruise missiles?
2. Will the limits be defined in terms of the range of cruise missiles—and if so, how will range be defined, since it is dramatically different at high versus low altitudes and fast versus slow speeds?

3. Do you protect against covert transfer of cruise missiles from other platforms by having the same limits on all types of cruise missiles?

A second and related factor is the extraordinary differences between the forces on the two sides; the forces are anything but mirror images of each other. As a consequence, when it gets down to negotiating about a particular verification problem, it is often not a mutual problem but rather one in which a particular system belonging to one side or the other has created the problem.

A third factor is the difference in verification assets. While both sides depend heavily on photoreconnaissance and other "spy" satellites, the Soviets have the back-up assurance of checking their intelligence data against Congressional testimony, U.S. newspaper articles, etc. There is no such open discussion of military systems in the Soviet Union.

How Much Do I Care: The Problem of Adequate Verification

Of crucial significance to any discussion of verification is the question of what constitutes "adequate verification." This question focuses on verifying quantitative limits such as permitted numbers of weapons, bans on weapons, ceilings on range, etc. The confidence level of one's observations is also a factor. For example, we might define "adequate verification" as plus or minus 5 percent for a critical limitation like the number of launchers of MIRVed ICBMs—whereas an uncertainty of plus or minus 50 percent (or even greater) might be acceptable for the range limit on cruise missiles launched from surface ships. The general criterion is that the uncertainty not undercut the objective of having the limit in the first place—and that any cheating not be of military significance.

The second concern, one's "confidence level," raises the question of "cheating." They wouldn't—or would they? The "they" is both sides, since it is clear that dependence on the element of trust has no place in an arms control negotiation between "enemies" who now only grudgingly accept that the requirements of achieving national security dictate that they limit their competition in weapons systems. It will be a long time—possibly generations—before the relationship between the U.S. and the Soviet Union would permit arms control limitations based on trust, as opposed to demanding verification requirements. Former President Ford once said that trust was earned, not given—a statement particularly appropriate to U.S.-Soviet arms control negotiation.

Spy in the Sky and Other Verification Techniques

In terms of the techniques for verification, the two sides to date have depended on independent assets (referred to as "national technical means of verification"—NTM) such as photoreconnaissance satellites and ships that collect data from missile tests over or near international waters. However, the two sides have nearly exhausted the set of systems (and limitations, save for reductions) for which "adequate verification" can be achieved through NTM, and it is this situation that presents the greatest challenge to the hopes for further progress in arms control.

In the U.S., the problem stems from our heavy dependence on photoreconnaissance satellites. The United States employs two types of photo satellites. The first uses the best film that Kodak can produce with capsules of film ejected out of orbit and picked out of the air as they descend by parachute over the Pacific. This film provides the best resolution of objects in the Soviet Union—good enough to distinguish between, say, men and woman (by dress) or Chevrolets and Cadillacs, but not good enough to distinguish bearded men from clean-shaven ones, or last year's Ford from this year's. The second type of U.S. satellite has a TV camera with resolution almost as good as the film and the advantage of always being there, scanning the Soviet Union many times a day. These, along with other intelligence collection satellites and systems, are extraordinary assets—but they're not good enough to monitor either the production or deployment of smaller weapons systems such as short-range cruise or ballistic missiles, torpedoes, etc. To achieve "adequate verification" of production limits or deployment limits on smaller systems, some type of cooperative efforts will be required—frequently expressed as a requirement for "on-site inspection."

The Soviet verification capability is nearly as good as that of the U.S., although they do not as yet possess the TV-type photoreconnaissance capability and their film is probably not as good as the best from Kodak.

On-Site Inspection: Are the Soviets Ready?

Not surprisingly, moving to the realm of "on-site inspection" and the implied presence of either gadgets (e.g., TV cameras) or personnel of the other side is sobering to both U.S. and Soviet government officials, but especially to the latter. The closed nature of Soviet society and the suspicion of any foreign elements are enormous roadblocks to the idea of revealing information about its military systems. One can well imagine their reaction to the idea of U.S. military personnel or UN observers with chalkboards and screwdrivers roaming around Soviet defense plants and military bases. But there is no question that, in the absence of a relationship built on a history of trust, that is the direction verification and arms control must go. And, to a small degree, it already has begun to do so.

In the 1974 negotiations on the Threshold Test Ban Treaty (TTBT) and the Peaceful Nuclear Explosive (PNE) Treaty, the long-time Soviet resistance and aversion to "on-site inspection" broke down, albeit to a very limited degree. To be specific, both of these treaties would permit on-site inspection in instances where other sources of information raise questions as to whether (1) a nuclear explosion exceeded the TTBT threshold (150 kilotons), or (2) a peaceful nuclear explosion had taken place. These were important steps for the Soviet Union to take, given its cultural aversion to the idea of foreigners having so intimate a view of activities internal to the country. Of potentially greater (albeit at this time still modest) significance was the Soviet agreement to permit U.S. "black boxes" (U.S. seismic monitoring stations that radio information to U.S. satellites) on Soviet nuclear test sites in the context of the Comprehensive Test Ban (CTB) negotiations.

In spite of the significance of these accomplishments, they are still a far cry from what will be needed to "adequately verify" a broader spectrum of limitations on the nuclear competition (e.g., a freeze on the production of short-range missiles.) In this context, three realms of on-site inspection (OSI) can be defined:

1. *OSI-1 (Mildly Intrusive).* U.S. black boxes at Soviet missile or nuclear weapons test sites; a U.S. option to challenge inspection in the case of ambiguous events, etc.

2. *OSI-2 (Very Intrusive)*. U.S. personnel outside Soviet factories or at Soviet test sites; random inspection at weapon deployment sites, etc.

3. *OSI-3 (Extraordinarily Intrusive)*. U.S. personnel inside certain Soviet factories or at certain military
   sites at all times, etc.

As indicated above, we have already entered the OSI-1
realm to a limited degree. Will the Soviets be willing to relax
their resistance to on-site inspection further to permit entering the OSI-2 realm, and maybe someday OSI-3? And is the
U.S. really ready for this kind of intrusion by Soviet personnel—as we would lead them to believe?

Soviet Treaty Violations—They Must Be Here Somewhere

One of the principal objectives of this book is to strip the
mystery and mythology from the Soviet Union and nuclear
war—and in this vein, one of the biggest myths of all is that
of Soviet treaty violations in the nuclear war realm.

If this book were devoted to an examination of every
agreement the Soviet government had signed since 1918—or
every treaty the U.S. government had signed since 1776—
the preceding statement might not be nearly as glib—or as
accurate. But the fact is, of the eight distinctive nuclear
weapons—related arms control agreements signed by the
Soviets in the nuclear age, there has not been a single charge
of a Soviet treaty violation by the U.S.—or vice versa (see
Exhibit 1). This statement remains the case as this book goes
to print at the beginning of the third year of the Reagan
administration, probably the most demanding administration
of the nuclear age in terms of its scrutiny of Soviet behavior.

The foregoing observation does not imply that there have
been no instances in which both sides have raised incidents
of ambiguous activities related to various agreed limitations.
In fact, under the SALT I agreements, a specific body, the
SALT Standing Consultative Commission, was established
to deal with such ambiguous activities[1]—and it has. Since
1972, the Commission, which continues to meet every six

---

[1]Article XIII of the ABM Treaty calls for establishment of a commission to "consider
questions concerning compliance with the obligations assumed and related situations
which may be considered ambiguous."

EXHIBIT 1
U.S.-Soviet Nuclear Arms Control Agreements

Agreement	Date of Signature	Charges of Violations
Limited Test Ban Treaty	1963	None
Non-Proliferation Treaty	1967	None
Outer Space Treaty	1968	None
SALT I ABM Treaty	1972	None
SALT I Interim Agreement	1972	None
Threshold Test Ban Treaty	1974	None
Peaceful Nuclear Explosions Treaty	1975	None
SALT II Treaty	1979	None

months, has handled in the vicinity of twenty issues relating to the SALT I agreements—with roughly two-thirds of these issues raised by the U.S. Every single one of these issues was resolved to the satisfaction of the challenging party.

In the context of examining the question of violations of the limitations in the various arms control treaties, it is also appropriate to examine the oft-cited violations of "the spirit" of an agreement. This accusation is often leveled at the Soviets by us—and at us by the Soviets. This issue—violations of the spirit of an agreement—is a red herring if ever there was one. If there's one thing that we in the United States should understand, in a complex world of free enterprise, contracts, lawyers and courts, it is the nonoperation and nonvalidity of the concept of "the spirit of an agreement."

Improved Relations: Horse Before Cart

The answer to the question of verification undoubtedly lies in the more basic question of the U.S.-Soviet relationship. Can that relationship be changed to the point where both sides believe that the other is committed to peaceful coexistence—the "Is this town big enough for both of us?" question? Until that question is answered, ambitious arms control limitations will remain the dream of technical experts and others who understand the complications of weapons systems and the challenge of insuring "adequate verification." Thus, more ambitious arms control agreements can be viewed as the cart that no longer is before the horse of improved U.S.-Soviet relations.

PART VI
The Prospects for a Great Leap Forward: The Future of U.S.-Soviet Relations

Chapter 21

Brezhnev's Successors: Will the Real Yuri Andropov Please Stand Up—Before It's Too Late!

In November 1982, Leonid Brezhnev, 75, for eighteen years General Secretary of the Communist Party of the Soviet Union and its unquestioned leader, suffered a heart seizure and died. Rumors of his failing health had been circulating throughout the West for well over five years, yet his death still came as a surprise both inside and outside the Soviet Union. Even more surprising was the speed with which Yuri Andropov was chosen his successor.

Unlike a Western democratic system, there is no established, public procedure for selecting a successor once a Soviet leader moves on. Formally, the Party Central Committee chooses the General Secretary. In practice, however, the Politburo chooses the successor, or at least has since Stalin, and submits its choice to the Central Committee for approval. In Novemeber 1982, defying the predictions of nearly every Western Sovietologist this procedure, which could take days or even weeks, took only a matter of hours. The new Party Secretary and Soviet leader would be Yuri Andropov, 68, formerly a longtime Politburo member and head of the KGB and now a member of the Party Secretariat. With equal surprise, he has moved rapidly to consolidate his power. How did all this happen and what does it mean for the future of the Soviet Union and the U.S.-Soviet relationship?

The Twilight of the Brezhnev Generation

The death of Brezhnev signaled the twilight of the Brezhnev generation. The advanced age of the current Soviet leadership at the time of his death—the average age of the Politburo was 70 (as compared to 56 in 1950, 58 in 1960 and 57 in 1966)—is a major factor in predicting the future course of Soviet political developments.

Men of Brezhnev's generation for the most part were young enough to remember but too young to have fought in the civil war. They were, however, old enough to have been exposed in their impressionable late teens and early twenties to the social, economic and intellectual ferment of the late 1920s. Many were Party members who were sent to college in the early 1930s (Brezhnev entered college in 1930 at the age of 23) to equip them to manage and control the administrative elites in the industrial and governmental bureaucracies. They had been promoted rapidly because of the purges and served a decade or more at middle- and upper-level positions under Stalin. In other words, these men have been at or near the top of the Soviet political hierarchy for 30 to 40 years.

The Transitional Generation

Yuri Andropov's generation—those individuals now in their sixties—have been waiting in the wings a long time. Born during and after World War I and the Russian Civil War, they are the Soviet Union's wartime generation whose ranks were decimated during World War II. In contrast to the U.S., those who were too young to receive a college education prior to the war did not return in droves in the postwar period. In a system where engineering and agronomy are the ranking academic disciplines, their mathematics and science background was too weak to compete with their younger colleagues. Instead, like Andropov, many went directly to work in Party cadres and other nontechnical positions. Because of wartime demands on the men, there are some women of this generation in responsible Party and administrative positions.

The Younger Generation: Coming to Power

Those individuals born in the Soviet Union after 1924 were the beneficiaries of a better primary and secondary education, a far lower chance of having their college education interrupted by the war and college entrance exams and standards that emphasized qualifications, not working class or peasant origins. Their career resumés appear quite normal by Western standards as they moved up the various bureaucratic ladders. For the majority, their careers began in the Cold War era and developed in the post-Stalin era of relaxed internal tensions, the beginnings of peaceful coexistence and contact with the West and, perhaps more importantly, the Soviet ascendance to parity with the U.S. in military capability. These developments could not help but have an impact on their view of their own country in relation to the U.S., the West and the world.

This upcoming generation of Soviet leaders with their backgrounds so different from the Brezhnev generation cannot help but have a different view of their country in relation to the U.S. and the rest of the world. Perhaps more importantly, they could very well offer more dynamic leadership and policy initiatives than the Brezhnev generation, which was characterized, especially in recent years, by a cautious, conservative approach to both foreign and domestic challenges. And their leader, chosen by the aging Brezhnev generation still in control of the Party Politburo, is Yuri Vladimirovich Andropov.

Yuri Vladimirovich Andropov

Yuri Vladimirovich Andropov, son of a railroad worker and now successor to Leonid Brezhnev as leader of the Soviet Union, was born on June 14, 1914 in the village of Nagutskoye, just north of the Caucasus Mountains in southwestern USSR. Unlike his predecessor (Brezhnev had been born in 1908), Andropov was too young at the time of the Russian Revolution and Civil War to have any recollection of those dramatic events. He was educated at the Rybinsk Water Transportation Technicum during the early years of Stalin's industrialization program and worked for a time as a telegraph operator and boatman on the Volga River. He attended Petrozavvodsk University briefly before dropping out in 1936 at the age of 22 to become an organizer for Komsomol, the Communist Party youth organization.

Andropov served as a political commissar with a Red Army unit at the Finnish front during World War II. In the late 1940s he occupied a series of local and regional Party Posts and developed a reputation as an expert on Eastern

Europe. As a result, he was then brought to Moscow in the early 1950s for further Party education that led to his assignment in 1954 as Soviet Ambassador to Hungary. While ambassador, he played a key role in the Soviet suppression of the 1956 Hungarian revolt, although the extent to which he was simply acting under orders from Moscow in this capacity remains uncertain. In 1957, Andropov was brought back from Hungary to head the Party Central Committee department in charge of relations with other Communist countries and in 1961 became a full member of the Central Committee Secretariat.

In 1967, the focus of Andropov's career changed when he was given the sensitive job of head of the Committee for State Security (KGB) at a time when the Party sought more stringent controls on internal dissent. Simultaneous with this appointment, he was moved from the Central Committee Secretariat to the Party Politburo, first as a nonvoting member, and then in 1973 with full membership. He was deliberate and pragmatic in executing his tasks, introducing incarceration in mental hospitals, expulsion and emigration as alternatives to the historic, and still extensively used, forced labor camps as the means of controlling dissenters. In his capacity as head of the KGB, he also presided over the extensive Soviet spy network.

With the death in the spring of 1982 of Mikhail Suslov, one of the most powerful members of the "collective leadership," Andropov was transferred from his position as head of the KGB to once again serve on the Party Secretariat, where he was given Suslov's position in charge of Party ideology, a responsibility of considerable prestige and power. In retrospect, many observers see this move as the beginning of an effort by a powerful faction within the Party leadership, including Defense Minister Ustinov and Foreign Minister Gromyko, to advance Andropov as a competitor to Brezhnev's apparent chosen successor, Konstantin Chernenko.

Thus, by the time of Brezhnev's death, Andropov, who had been considered a dark horse candidate as recently as the spring of 1982, was now seen to be locked in a head-to-head run with Chernenko. When Andropov was chosen to head the 25-man board that planned Brezhnev's funeral, many people sensed correctly that the job would be his. But few expected that the transition and his formal selection would take place so quickly, leading many to speculate that the choice had been made by Kremlin power brokers some time before Brezhnev's death.

Andropov the Man: "Charming, but Brutal"

In part because of relative obscurity during his 15-year tenure as head of the KGB, little is known about Yuri Andropov beyond his basic career path and a few fragments from those who have met and known him. For example, although he presided over the Soviet suppression of the Hungarian revolt, he is also remembered as someone who took the time to learn the Hungarian language and culture in his three-year stay there. He is believed to speak some English, a rarity among Party leaders, although his discussions with Vice President Bush and Secretary of State Shultz at the time of Brezhnev's funeral were all conducted through interpreters. He is also believed to have an interest in American popular culture, including collecting American popular music records and reading American popular novels. He is a widower with a son and daughter.

Andropov's political orientation appears particularly clouded to outside observers. His roles in Hungary and the KGB suggest an autocratic orientation characteristic of past Soviet leaders, but he is often portrayed by his image makers (like American leaders, Soviet leaders also have "image makers") as a "closet liberal" open to political and economic reform.

As head of the KGB for 15 years, Andropov is probably better informed about the U.S. and how it thinks and operates than any previous Soviet leader. He also has close ties to Georgi Arbatov, head of the Institute of the USA and Canada and one of his chief advisors in the 1960s. (Andropov's son also works for Arbatov's Institute.) He praised détente in speeches long after other Soviet leaders were denouncing the U.S. but has aligned himself strongly with the Soviet military, taking a position in opposition to Chernenko on the question of diverting funds from military expenditures to the consumer sector. Yet his orientation toward the U.S. and relations with the West seem particularly uncertain. In his first speech as the Soviet Union's new leader, for example, Andropov observed, "We know full well that the imperialists will never meet one's plea for peace. It can be upheld only by relying on the invincible might of the Soviet armed forces." Yet a few days later, after making similar statements at Brezhnev's funeral with Vice President Bush and Secretary of State Shulz in attendance, he noted, "We are always ready for honest, equal and mutually beneficial cooperation with any state that is willing to cooperate." His talks with these U.S. representatives the next day were said to be constructive, and Soviet Premier Tikhonov, the head of the government bureaucracy, responded to President Reagan's message of condolence on the death of Leonid Brezhnev by saying, "The Soviet Union has been and is for normal, and even better, friendly relations with the United States of America. There were such relations in the past and they can again become a reality."

In his various administrative positions, Andropov has developed a reputation as a pragmatist and a tough man to work for. He is described as highly energetic, decisive and performance-oriented, demanding a great deal of himself and his subordinates. He is known to have some health problems, however: he has had at least one heart attack, has very bad eyesight and is thought to be a diabetic. These problems and his age—68 at the time he took office—have led some observers to suggest his will be a transitional leadership.

The Man

In sum, Andropov comes to the position as leader of the Soviet Union without having given any clear signals to outside observers as to the kind of leader he will be or the kind of policies he will pursue. His rise to the top position marks him as a person with powerful friends within the Party leadership, and as someone who knows how to play the game of Party politics effectively. But his past may not be the key element in defining the "Andropov era," or defining how long that era will last. That key element may well be the weight and urgency of the problems facing the Soviet Union as he takes the reins of power. The most pressing of the problems that confront the man the *Wall Street Journal* described as "charming but brutal" are described in the following chapter.

Chapter 22

Red Skies at Morning: Forces for Change on the Soviet Horizon

The ancient mariners had an expression, "Red skies at night, sailor's delight; red skies at morning, sailors take warning." Imagine, if you will, waking up one morning and gazing out to the horizon and the sky is red. Imagine, if you will, waking up one morning and being told you've just been chosen as the leader of the Soviet Union. Imagine you are Yuri Andropov. What would you do?

Although the long-awaited Brezhnev succession has now taken place and Yuri Andropov has assumed the Party leadership, there is still a general consensus that the Soviet Union is not about to undertake a major change of structure and approach to its many pressing problems at least until Andropov and other members of the new leadership have consolidated their power. These problems are very real, however, and in many cases must be confronted in the very near term. In this chapter we review these problems and the alternative future scenarios they suggest for the next decade or more in the Soviet Union.

The Forces of Change

The forces for change in the Soviet Union can be loosely grouped into three categories:

(1) *Political Forces,* which include (a) transition to a new political leadership, and (b) movement toward greater institutional pluralism in the Soviet political system, most importantly in the growing demands of other elites (military, technical and managerial) that the Party *apparat* surrender their monopoly of political power;

(2) *Economic Forces,* which include (a) decreasing effectiveness of Stalinist-type central planning, (b) decreasing availability and rising costs of the factors of production, (c) declining productivity, and (d) resulting pressure on the macro-level allocation among consumption, defense and capital investment; and

(3) *Social and Cultural Forces,* which include (a) resurgence of religious and nationalist (Russian and non-Russian) sentiments, and (b) demographic changes.

Political Forces

As already noted, the dominant variable in the political arena is the conclusion of the Brezhnev era and the transition to a new regime. Andropov's ascendance to the leadership of the Party and nation is of critical importance, in terms of his personality, background and ideological predisposition. But it is also important whether or not his role is that of chairman of a collective leadership or that of a dominant leader characteristic of the latter years of the Stalin, Khrushchev and Brezhnev eras.

A collective leadership is almost certain to be more inclined toward a conservative approach to meeting political and economic challenges, given the need for consensus in group decision-making. In contrast, a dominant leader would be freer to move the country in new directions and toward major reforms. The results could be a country oriented toward high-risk adventures on either the foreign or domestic front. This could be both good and bad—good, for example, if the initiatives were aggressive, such as in the arms control area, reducing the risk of nuclear war; bad if they would mean challenging the U.S. head-on at critical places around the globe.

The new leadership is expected by most analysts to be a collective leadership in the short run. Andropov does not yet have the stature within the Party or nation to command the authority of a Brezhnev, much less a Stalin, although eventually he could emerge as such a leader.

A second political force is the pressure on the Party *apparat* to share some of its authority with other elites within the Soviet political system. These pressures come from many quarters and take many forms, including the military, who want more of a say in defense and foreign policy, and technical-managerial elites and intellectuals who want more of a say in their particular areas of Party and governmental decision-making.

A final although significantly less potent force for change in the Soviet political system comes from national minorities wanting more autonomy for their union republics and more of a say in Party and government decision-making that affects their regions.

Economic Forces

As outlined in Chapter 7, the era of high and continuous annual growth rates in the Soviet economy appears to be at an end. Both current annual growth (1 to 2 percent) and the projections of growth for the 1981–85 Five-Year Plan (3.4 percent) are the lowest in Soviet history. This slowdown in growth will exacerbate an already difficult problem of allocating national income among consumption, defense and capital investment in industry and agriculture.

One of the most fundamental and far-reaching forces for change is the growing realization that the system of Stalinist-type central planning that produced fairly rapid economic growth in the 1930s and 1950s is no longer effective in the more developed and complex Soviet economy of the 1970s and 1980s. Economists pinpoint the problem as one of moving from a period of extensive (increased *quantity* of inputs) to intensive (increased *quality* of inputs), growth, presenting different management problems. This highlights the second set of forces at work in bringing Soviet economic growth close to a halt—declining inputs of the factors of production and the declining productivity of those factors.

The number of new workers entering the Soviet labor force will decline precipitously throughout the 1980s, in part of a legacy of the millions of young men and women lost in the 1941–45 period. Production of energy resources and key commodities is relatively stagnant and in some instances declining. This overall decline is magnified by the stagnation in productivity, especially of Soviet capital inputs, and the demands of the defense and consumer sectors, which continue to leave a small part of the national income available for reinvestment. Finally, agriculture remains a serious problem, requiring the expenditure of huge amounts of scarce hard currency despite the fact that the government is pouring approximately one-third of the nation's total capital investment into it in an effort to increase domestic output.

Overwhelmingly, these economic problems are amplified by the existing economic bureaucracy that hinders efficiency and innovation in both planning and execution of the plan. The planning system, while struggling with redirecting and managing resources at the macro level, faces a major problem with the heavy operational emphasis of the plan at the micro (plant) level. Plant managers have little freedom of action or incentive to pioneer innovations, making economic reform difficult. Moreover, central planners don't have enough information to do efficiently the job that plant managers should be doing, and there is a shortage of good, well-trained managers.

The normal interdependence of sectors of any socio-economic system complicates matters further. For example, increased agricultural productivity requires increased capital investment, which requires available capital, which requires economic growth, which requires greater productivity, which requires greater incentives for workers, which requires, among other things, more and better food, which requires greater agricultural productivity. It is a difficult cycle to break and reform once it is out of synchronization.

The significance of Soviet economic problems is not limited to the economic sector. These problems have serious political consequences, some of which have already been noted:

- The need to import modern technology and grain, in many instances from potential adversaries, such as the U.S. and Western Europe;
- The impact of the declining growth rate and demands of other sectors on defense spending;
- The consequences of supplying or not supplying Eastern Europeans with energy and raw materials now in short supply in the Soviet Union;
- The internal competition among ministries in an era of resource scarcity;
- The exacerbation of problems with the Muslim and Turkic minorities if it becomes advantageous to move sizeable numbers of them to distant industrial locations.

Of these factors, perhaps the most significant is the economic impact of defense spending.

The Soviet defense budget is slightly higher than that of the United States in an economy half its size.[1] Thus the drain on societal resources—specialized labor, engineers, scientists, management, capital, machinery, parts and raw materials—is that much greater, especially because the Soviet industrial system has a much smaller high-technology base than do the industrial systems of the U.S. and other Western countries.

Overall, there appears to be a consensus among Western economists that major economic reforms are necessary in the planning and management of the Soviet economy before an increase in growth rates above present levels can be reestablished. These reforms focus on the micro level, where substantial incentives for innovation and efficiency of operations and a longer-term perspective must be introduced into the plan. Regrettably, it is difficult to change, much less radically alter, a system that has been historically stable and productive *in its time*, and that has built a system of influence, power and prestige among the cadres that operate and support it.

Social and Cultural Forces

The social and cultural forces with the greatest potential for bringing changes in the Soviet Union are the revivals of religion and nationalism among the various indigenous groupings within the society. In contrast to Poland, however, the religious revival in the Soviet Union has not yet developed any political overtones. Even if it should, it is doubtful that it would have the capacity to displace Marxism-Leninism as the guiding dogma in the society, although it could diminish its power and significance.

The pressures of the various nationality groups are potentially more serious, especially if the Soviet Union were to experience severe economic or political problems. If this were to be the case, and the national government were

---

[1] The CIA estimates the Soviet defense budget to be 50 percent higher, but as noted in Chapter 7, comparability is difficult and some experts believe the CIA estimates are unjustifiably high.

severely weakened, some observers believe that these minority nationalities would demand more autonomy for themselves, or, at the extreme, would attempt to break free of the Soviet Union and reestablish themselves as independent states. But Soviet minority groups, especially those who are educated, have not been systematically blocked from some measure of upward mobility and improved living standards, as has often been the case with minorities elsewhere. As a result, revolutionary sentiment within these minority groups is not large, although it could become a potent force in certain areas, for example in the Baltic states.

A final and very significant concern is the possibility of a revival of a militant fundamentalism, possibly Communism but more likely Russian nationalism. Although the increasing diversity of the Soviet population and the growth of the technical-managerial suggests the development of a militant fundamentalism does not seem likely, many analysts believe that Russian nationalism or chauvinism is a highly potent force waiting to be released, a force that at various times in history—World War II, for example—has rallied the Russian people to great achievements.

Alternative Scenarios for the Soviet Future

In 1969, Andrei Amalrik, a young Soviet historian living in Moscow, wrote a lengthy essay entitled, "Will the Soviet Union Survive until 1984?," a question he answered in the negative.[2] Amalrik argued that the expansionist tendencies in the Soviet elite would lead them into a disastrous war with China, after which the Soviet Union would either (1) fall into chaos and possibly follow the course of Rome, or (2) become a loose confederation similar to the European Common Market.

In 1970, the same year that Amalrik's essay was published in the U.S., American Sovietologist Zbigniew Brzezinski drew the future of the Soviet Union in far less apocalyptic terms. Brzezinski saw the Soviet leadership striking a balance between the perpetuation of the existing system with increasing ideological intensity and accommodation to the demands for more emphasis on technological innovation and

---

[2]Andrei Amalrik, *Will the Soviet Union Survive until 1984?* (New York: Harper Colophon, 1970). Amalrik hedged his argument somewhat before his death in 1982.

power for themselves from the new technical and managerial elite.[3]

As we enter 1983, none of the steps toward Amalrik's catastrophic conclusion have occurred as yet. In fact, Brzezinski's 1970 scenario seems far closer to the mark. Following Andropov's succession of Brezhnev, the current Soviet regime appears stable, despite the increasing tensions surrounding the list of problems and strains outlined above. Although many leading Sovietologists have been reluctant to engage in predicting alternative scenarios for the future of the Soviet Union, some have joined Amalrik and Brzezinski over the past decade. An inventory of the offerings includes:

Revolution
Progressive degeneration and decay
Development of an authoritarian Great Russian state
A military coup and dictatorship
Neo-Stalinism
Transfer of power to the technocrat-managerial stratum
Convergence with the Western system
Liberalization and democratization of the system
Socialist democracy and worker self-management
Ethical-religious rebirth
Limited modernization of the existing system
Continuation of the system unchanged[4]

Despite the temptation toward prediction and the seeming logic of extrapolating current trends and forces for change into the future, the reticence of many leading Sovietologists to predict the future of the Soviet Union seems appropriate. There are simply too many known variables interwoven in complex forms before even considering the "unknown unknowns"—the accidents of history, unrevealed personality characteristics, unexpected crises—to bet the grocery money on a political scenario for the future of the Soviet Union. Nevertheless, it is the knowledge of what has gone before and the major variables that bear watching that will enable us to stay close to change as it does occur in the Soviet Union, and make whatever adjustments can be made in the U.S.-Soviet relationship.

3Zbigniew Brzezinski, *Between Two Ages* (New York: Viking Press, 1970), pp. 167–68.
4Seweryn Bialer, *Stalin's Successors* (New York: Cambridge University Press, 1981), p. 283.

Chapter 23

Lifting Each Other by the Bootstraps: U.S.-Soviet Cooperative Efforts

Given the current strains in the U.S.-Soviet relationship and the lack of progress in arms controls talks over the past few years, one has to wonder if there are other means whereby communication and cooperation between the two superpowers might be reestablished. Early signals from the new Andropov regime suggest that the Soviet Union may be interested in making the effort. What avenues are available?

Paralleling the SALT I agreements, the brief era of détente in the early 1970s saw a substantial effort to establish cooperation and exchange programs between the two countries in three broad categories: science and technology, trade and culture. While many of the programs showed considerable promise for improving U.S.-Soviet communication and cooperation, like SALT, most have fallen victim to the acrimonious atmosphere that has enveloped the U.S.-Soviet relationship in recent years. Nevertheless, an exploration of these experiences is a good basis on which to begin to examine the potential pitfalls should the two superpowers once again embark on a multidimensional effort at improved relations and détente.

Hope in the Universality of Science

Scientific exchange and cooperation programs between the United States and the Soviet Union began in 1958, more than a decade before President Nixon's 1972 visit to Moscow inaugurated the period of U.S.-Soviet détente. They had been sustained since 1959 by a series of two-year agreements between the two governments, with the U.S. role administered first by the National Academy of Sciences

(NAS), and since 1968, through the International Research and Exchange Program (IREX), both nongovernmental but government-supported agencies.

Prior to 1958, only a handful of American scholars had worked in the Soviet Union, and that was from 1924 to 36; no Americans at all had studied in Soviet universities from 1936 to 58. Between 1958 and 1975, however, more than a thousand American scholars spent an average of three months in the Soviet Union, generally at either Moscow or Leningrad State University.

At the Nixon-Brezhnev summit meetings in Moscow in 1972 and Washington in 1973, bilateral exchange and cooperation agreements were also signed that promised to greatly increase the flow of scientific exchange between the U.S. and the Soviet Union in such areas as health, space, environmental protection, agriculture, transportation, oceanography, peaceful uses of atomic energy, energy, housing and construction, and science and technology generally. Of these programs, those in environmental protection, science and technology, health, energy and atomic energy drew the largest number of man-months of exchange. In 1977, over 700 American scientists visited the Soviet Union as a part of the agreements, although most were for periods of two weeks or less.

The panel governing the exchanges acknowledged that, taking all fields together, the U.S. scientific capability was clearly stronger than that of the Soviet Union, and while some leading American scientists argued that little could be gained from the exchanges, the majority felt that even in those areas where the Soviet Union lagged, the U.S. could benefit from the exchange. They also felt that the most important goal of the program from their perspective—the fostering of an international scientific community which they hoped would be accompanied by an easing of U.S.-Soviet tensions—was being advanced by the exchanges.

The exchange program has been criticized by some scientists for giving legitimacy to the Soviet regime and repressive political conditions in the country. Other critics of the exchanges charge that they offer an opportunity for a "rip-off" of U.S. high technology by the Soviets. In the areas of science, well removed from technology applications, this problem does not seem to occur, however. The exception is where scientific instrumentation is involved and in areas such as lasers and semiconductors, where the gap between fundamental and applied research is small; but in both areas the exchanges are tightly controlled. It is a more serious problem in trade and commercial exchanges, as discussed below.

The sensitivity of American scientists to the political fate of their counterparts in the Soviet Union—Andrei Sakharov, for example—highlights some of the difficulties of the exchange program for that country. The Soviet Union very much wants and needs access to American know-how in a variety of areas and sees the scientific exchange and cooperation programs as one means of achieving it. However, it knows that greater intercourse with the West could undermine support for the current regime by those participants who come in contact with the more free and open scientific environment of the West.

A Sample Program: Cooperation in Space

The brief history of the agreement for cooperation in space, which the U.S. and Soviet Union signed in 1972, is characteristic of the hope, problems and disappointments in scientific exchanges. Working groups were established immediately in space meteorology, environmental studies, lunar and planetary exploration, and space biology and medicine. The high point of the cooperative effort was the Soyuz-Apollo linkup in space in July 1975, when two Soviet cosmonauts and three American astronauts crawled through a tunnel connecting their two spacecraft and transmitted to earthbound television viewers in the U.S. and Soviet Union handshakes and shared meals.

Over the next two years, space agency officials from the two countries met frequently to discuss possible follow-up programs. But in the fall of 1977, the meetings ceased with the cooling of U.S.-Soviet relations over the human rights issue, and the Carter Administration's sensitivity to charges that the U.S. was giving away more scientific and technical information than it was getting.

Plans for cooperation in two other areas—the exchange of meteorological data from weather satellites and remote sensing data, primarily from Landsat missions—also were shelved. The only areas where cooperation was maintained were space biology and planetary science. Under the planetary science agreement, the two countries exchanged moon rocks and the U.S. provided radar maps of Venus for a Soviet mission to that planet in early 1982 in exchange for data from the missions. In space biology, the U.S. supplied instruments in exchange for data from a Soviet program that put test animals in space in the late 1970s.

In June 1982, however, the Reagan Administration called a halt to cooperative efforts in space when it allowed the U.S.-Soviet space cooperation agreement, which had last been renewed in 1977, to expire without renewal. A number of minor cooperative efforts not dependent on the agreement would continue, but any major efforts were over. Thus, U.S.-Soviet space cooperation joined the fate of the programs on cooperation in science and technology and energy, which the Reagan Administration had shelved as part of sanctions announced in response to the imposition of martial law in Poland in late 1981. (Agreements in environmental protection, oceanography, atomic energy and medical science for development of an artificial heart had been renewed in November 1981 just before the martial law decree in Poland, and remained in effect.) In summary, there were some fruitful cooperative efforts in the brief era of détente, but performance fell far short of the original promise, and the overall objective of the free exchange of information and ideas remained an elusive goal.

East-West Trade: "Sell Them Anything They Can't Shoot Back at Us"[1]

Quite by circumstance, at the same time as foreign dignitaries from around the globe gathered in Moscow in November 1982 for the funeral of Leonid Brezhnev, executives from over 200 American corporations were also meeting in Moscow with Nikolai S. Patilochev, Soviet Minister for Foreign Trade, and other representatives of Soviet ministries to discuss the possibility of renewed trade between the two countries. The occasion was the first meeting in four years of the U.S.-USSR Trade and Economic Council, which had been set up in 1973 by Patolichev and George P. Shultz, then U.S. Secretary of Commerce and now Secretary of State.

---

[1] A comment on trade with the Soviet Union attributed to President Dwight Eisenhower.

The meeting had been convened to explore the forms of trade still possible given the various sanctions that had been applied by the U.S. in the Carter and Reagan Administrations, and so the companies in attendance represented primarily such industries as agricultural products and equipment, food processing, chemicals and commercial goods. During the sessions, Soviet officials stressed two points to the Americans in attendance: (1) that it was futile for the U.S. to try to blockade the Soviet economy, and (2) that, in Patolichev's words, "It is necessary for the United States to renounce once and for all the doctrine of using trade as a weapon against our country" if trade between the two countries was ever going to improve.

Indeed, U.S.-Soviet trade was at its lowest level in years. Since 1979, the U.S. share of machinery imports to the Soviet Union had fallen from 7 percent to 3 percent, and grain imports from 71 percent to 17 percent. Even though the Reagan Administration used the conference as an opportunity to lift the sanctions against U.S. companies whose technology was being sold or licensed for use on the Siberia-Western European natural gas pipeline, it seemed determined to move back toward the strategy of offensive economic warfare against the Soviet Union that had characterized U.S. policy during the cold war.

This policy had begun to give way in the mid-1960s as the Soviet government adopted a conscious policy of technology transfer from the West, leading first Western European and then U.S. firms to actively pursue sales of their products in the Soviet Union and Eastern Europe. In the early 1970s, spurred on by détente, the U.S. government adopted a "qualified free trade approach" to U.S.-Soviet trade, permitting the sale of "resource-freeing" products (products that would enable the Soviet Union to develop and more efficiently utilize its natural resources) to the Soviet Union but seeking to delay Soviet "capability enhancement" in high technology.

In support of a freer trade policy, Henry Kissinger argued that whereas a strong industrial base remained essential in a conventional war where protracted conflict would occur, in the era of nuclear war the conflict would be brief, and a few specialized industries and scientific know-how would be decisive and their importance would precede the conflict.

On this basis he argued that ". . . there is no necessary relationship between economic strength and military strength."[2] In support of freer trade, others argued that neither the Soviet Union nor any nation would be foolish enough to base its national security on external sources of strategic technology, especially from a potential adversary.

Even at the height of U.S.-Soviet trade in the mid-1970s, substantial restrictions remained on the transfer of vital technology that could have military application through a series of lists and control procedures. First, each Western nation had its own list (in the U.S. it is known as the U.S. Commodity Control list). Coordination among Western nations is maintained through the Coordinating Committee for Export Controls (COCOM). Control of the U.S. list and the granting of exemptions when deemed acceptable is in the hands of the Secretary of State, but other government agencies participate through the Economic Defense Advisory Committee (EDAC).

The basic U.S. approach to trade with the Soviet Union emphasizes national security considerations over potential economic benefits. This approach is in sharp contrast to that of its European allies, who favor depoliticization of trade. The West Germany policy of *Osthandel* (trade with the East), for example, emphasizes a positive linkage between trade and East-West relations and rejects such negative linkages as using trade to punish the Soviet Union for its policies and actions. Although they acknowledge the need to embargo exports of military technology, the West Germans believe COCOM needs to be reformed and made less cumbersome.

The European focus on the positive linkage between increased trade and improvement in East-West relations also has its advocates in the U.S. In attacking the Reagan Administration's use of the provisions of the Export Administration Act to limit trade with the Soviet Union, Robert Schmidt, President of the American Committee on East-West Accord and Vice Chairman of the Board of Control Data Corporation, argued:

2Henry Kissinger, *Nuclear Weapons and Foreign Policy* (New York: Harper Brothers, 1973), p. 2.

. . . [O]ur present attitude toward the Soviet Union considerably enhances the risk of mutual annihilation. I would not be so simplistic as to argue that a restoration of trade with the Russians could eliminate that risk. But I do argue that trade, and the increased opportunities for communication that go with trade and a growing interdependence will substantially reduce the risk.

The Excessive Debt of the Soviet Bloc

One final factor that may prove an even greater roadblock to East-West trade than the restrictive policies of the Reagan administration is the growing debt to the West of the Soviet Union and the countries of Eastern Europe. This debt is the product of the aggressive lending policy of Western bankers in a decade in which imports substantially exceed exports for most Soviet bloc countries. Poland, for example, owes Western nations $25 billion and the Soviet Union owes $20 billion. As a result, after doubling during the 1970s, East-West trade flattened out in 1979 and now has slightly fallen, with little prospect for a major change, despite the optimism of participants in the Moscow trade meetings in November 1982.

Folks Meeting Folks: Cultural Exchange

Like scientific exchange and trade, cultural exchange between the Soviet Union and the U.S. was given a significant promotional boost in the early 1970s with the beginnings of détente. The promise was not only for a series of exchange visits involving performing artists and performing companies, but also for genuine people-to-people exchanges that might begin to establish a basis for better communication and understanding between Soviet and American citizens. As with scientific exchange and trade, however, the achievements of cultural exchange never came close to meeting expectations. By the early 1980s even the limited program of cultural exchange undertaken had fallen victim to the soured relations between the two countries. With this handicap, the natural roadblocks to culture exchange—economic, in that the cost of sending Soviet citizens to the U.S. must be paid in hard currency since the ruble has no foreign exchange value, and political, the extreme caution of the Soviet government and local politicians in the U.S.—could not be overcome.

The Estranged Sister Cities

One of the programs that grew out of détente was a pilot study involving the establishment of sister city relationships between five U.S. and Soviet cities, coordinated by Sister Cities International in the U.S. and the Soviet Society of Friendship in the Soviet Union. The cities, with their Soviet counterparts, were:

Seattle, Washington, and Tashkent, an industrial center in the Moslem area of Southwestern Siberia;

Baltimore, Maryland, and Odessa, a Black Sea port in the southern Ukraine;

Oakland, California, and Nakhodka, a Pacific Ocean port in the Soviet Far East;

Houston, Texas, and Baku, a major oil refining center on the Caspian Sea;

Jacksonville, Florida, and Murmansk, the Soviet port on the Arctic Ocean through which much of the Lend-Lease aid granted by the U.S. to the Soviet Union during World War II passed.

Of these sister city relationships, only four ever involved any people exchange at all. The Baltimore-Odessa relationship was quashed by the objection of expatriot Ukrainians living in Baltimore before any exchange at all took place. The Houston-Baku and Jacksonville-Murmansk exchanges involved small delegations headed by the respective mayors, making single visits each way. Then in early 1980, the Soviet invasion of Afghanistan led the mayors of the two U.S. cities to shelve the program.

The Seattle-Tashkent relationship, although it also involved only small delegations going in either direction, was still alive in early 1982, when a Soviet delegation headed by the Tashkent mayor visited Seattle. Later in 1982, as part of a citywide nuclear war education exercise designed to show the impact of a nuclear attack on Seattle, a Seattle organization extended contact with Tashkent. The Oakland-

Nakhodka relationship is also still active, although it has never gone beyond the exchange of delegations from the respective port commissions discussing matters relating exclusively to port management.

In sum, the hope of establishing people-to-people communication through a system of sister cities relationships never made any significant progress, even in the pilot study.

Tourism: The Unrealized Potential

Détente brought an acceleration of East-West tourism, with an average of 30,000 Americans a year visiting the Soviet Union. Visits were largely limited to Moscow and Leningrad and a handful of other cities, however, since many Soviet cities are off-limits to foreign tourists. Although the total number of Soviet citizens visiting the U.S. also increased significantly after 1972, rising from 2800 Soviet visitors in 1972 to 6,000 a year by 1979, these visits also fell off in the early 1980s to only 4,000 Soviet citizens in total.

Sliding to the Bottom with Détente

U.S.-Soviet scientific cooperation hangs on by a thread. U.S.-Soviet trade, handicapped by its use as a policy tool as much as by national security considerations, is near its lowest level in a decade. Because of economic and political constraints in the Soviet Union and the pressures of domestic politics in the U.S., cultural exchanges have made no significant contribution in fostering U.S.-Soviet cooperation. In sum, U.S.-Soviet cooperative and exchange efforts, stranded in the same rut as arms control and détente, have no direction to go but up.

Afterword

Is This Blue Marble Big Enough for the Both of Us? The Future of U.S.-Soviet Relations

The man who led the Soviet Union for eighteen years is dead. A new man has taken his place. He assumes leadership of a nation whose problems, both foreign and domestic, are as enormous as the country itself. He also inherits a relationship of enmity with the other global superpower—the United States. In both countries, prospects for the future of the relationship remain uncertain, tied as they are to long-standing conflicts both in terms of ideology and in terms of interests. Yet the two are indissolubly linked, not simply by their conflicts, but also by the challenge represented by the vast arsenals of destruction that both possess, arsenals with which they could destroy each other and possibly life on the earth itself. And so each must confront the same question, as they seek solutions to those conflicts that divide them: is the earth—that Big Blue Marble—big enough for the both of us?

The foregoing chapters have sought to show the historical and present condition of the Soviet Union and the U.S.-Soviet relationship. The historical picture is one with roots deep in the Russian past, and more shallowly set in events of the twentieth century—the Revolution, the hot wars, the cold war and, more recently, the mutual U.S. and Soviet efforts to find ways of defusing the strains that developed in their relationship in the postwar period. In this recent past, we have seen the Soviet Union build a massive strategic and conventional military capability as it sought to develop a favorable relationship with the U.S. through the process of détente, and in particular through arms control. Soviet objectives in this period have not varied significantly, seeking as they have equality with the U.S., global stature and security to pursue policies and actions that would advance their desire to lead the socialist world, secure the power of the Communist party at home and maintain their effective control over Eastern Europe.

The U.S. response to Soviet policies and actions in this period, in contrast to the continuity in the Soviet Union, has more closely resembled the movement of a yoyo, changing as each new Administration took office, and changing in response to particular Soviet moves. Thus we have gone from SALT I to the Jackson-Vanik Amendment, from SALT II to the grain embargo and failure of ratification, from hard-line, cold-war rhetoric to the lifting of the grain embargo, from START proposals to economic embargoes—responding impulsively, both for emotional and domestic political reasons, to the variations in Soviet actions rather than to the essential problems in the U.S.-Soviet relationship. These vacillations speak to a fundamental problem in this country—a lack of understanding, if not downright ignorance, of the Soviet Union and its significance for the United States and its place in the world, a lack of understanding that many people, both in policymaking circles and the general public, would seem to want to perpetuate for ideological reasons. If there has been any consistency in our posture towards the Soviet Union, it has been in our underlying attitudes, not in our policies and actions.

The massive Soviet military buildup over the past 15 years (the buildup has actually been underway almost since the time of the Revolution and certainly since 1928) has been accompanied by a decline in the country's political, economic and social climate. The economy is sputtering under the heavy drain of defense expenditures, made worse by declining availability of natural resources, labor, investment capital and the increasing demand of Soviet consumers for a better diet and more consumer goods. Dissent, while quashed by the KGB, is only the tip of the iceberg, not of revolutionary sentiment but of a Soviet public that seems to have lost its ideological commitment to the ideals of a communist state. While most still support their government, they increasingly lead their private lives separate from the public world of tired Marxist-Leninist sloganeering, hoping for more meat and fewer government intrusions in their daily existence.

But these are only symptoms of a general malaise, a problem Yuri Andropov has given indications he recognizes only too well. But there are even more important currents still. The Soviet Union today is struggling with an identity crisis, one that has been going on since the nineteenth century, if not since Peter the Great: do they want to be a part of the Western world, with its bourgeois decadence and political liberalism, or do they want to retreat back to their xenophobic, autarkic past, isolated from the West but in touch with their noble Slavic roots. This conflict is being played out in the Soviet Union today among factions that represent both points of view, as well as in the minds of individual Soviet citizens, perhaps even including Yuri Andropov himself.

As we set our course for dealing with the Soviet Union in the future, we have an opportunity to influence only in a very modest way the outcome of this internal Soviet debate. While we may not be able to advance the case of those who would seek to turn the country toward détente with the West, we can by our actions play into the hands of the xenophobic Slavophiles who have always been suspicious of the outside world and in particular the United States and would willingly drop the Iron Curtain tomorrow and reestablish Stalin's autarkic "Fortress Russia." Instead, our objective should be to make clear to the new Soviet leadership the limits of our tolerance for Soviet actions and our own view as to where bridges between our two countries could be built anew, rather than burned, as seems to have been our orientation recently. If the history of the Soviet past has told us anything, it is that there are substantial limitations to the impact we can have on Soviet policy—we can perhaps limit their options, but we cannot dictate policy choices.

In this vein the future should be viewed as offering opportunities for mutual progress towards finding ways that we can both live on the Big Blue Marble together—ways in which "two can tango," to paraphrase President Reagan—not for confrontation and exploitation of our respective weaknesses. It should also offer opportunities to move away from a generation of mutual suspicion and varying degrees of hard-line, cold war rhetoric in which pronouncements on both sides are cast exclusively in terms of "(we're) right and (they're) wrong." We can choose to stay that course, but it offers no long-term solutions and could be a prescription for disaster.

Whatever course we choose to follow, progress is certain to come slowly. While our confrontation with the Soviet Union is little more than 35 years old, the roots of our respective societies go back centuries. They are fundamentally different roots, giving rise to different cultures, political, social and economic systems, and military policies and even weaponry. Those differences are not going to be breached in the short run, if they ever can be at all.

In closing, we acknowledge that events of the future could outrun and deny the logic of the arguments for greater understanding presented in this book, bringing us to the brink of nuclear war. If, by some divine intercession, a single wish is granted at that last pre-Armageddon moment to those who care deeply for the fate of the Big Blue Marble, let their wish be this: that in that crisis, as the two sides prepare to move toward their certain mutual destruction, the first two missiles fired should also carry the leaders of both nations into a rendezvous in space. Then, just as their missiles are about to "go ballistic," after which neither will be able to control their flight, let them turn back to view the Big Blue Marble and see a universally familiar face appear at their windows saying, "Yuri Vladimirovich Andropov and Ronald Wilson Reagan, Zvaneé damóy . . . Call home!"

Appendix 1

COMPARATIVE ECONOMIC AND OTHER DATA
FOR
THE UNITED STATES AND THE SOVIET UNION

I. Geography	United States	Soviet Union
Area (millions of square miles)	3.62	8.65
Miles of land frontier	5,200	10,500
Population (millions of persons)	226	267
Urbanization	73.5%	62.0%

II. Social Conditions		
Birth rate (per 1,000 population)	15.0	17.7
Infant mortality (per 1,000 live births)	14.0	27.7
Life expectancy: Men/Women (years)	69/77	64/74
Literacy	99%	99%

III. The Economic System		
Gross National Product (GNP) ($Trillion, 1980)	2.6	1.5
GNP per capita	$9,810	$5,730
Growth rate, GNP (1950–75)	3.3%	5.3%
Growth rate, GNP (1980)	.2%	1.5%
Trade, exports plus imports ($Billion, 1980)	461	145
National defense expenditures (% of GNP)	5%	11-14% est.
National defense expenditures ($Billion, 1980)	136	160-210 est.
Production of automobiles (millions, 1980)	6.4	2.2
Consumption of dairy products (lbs per capita)	290	690
Consumption of meat (lbs. per capita)	201	126
Television sets (millions in use)	121	60
Telephones (millions in use)	162	20
Automobiles (millions in use)	150	7

TRADE BETWEEN THE SOVIET UNION AND THE U.S.

	U.S. Exports to the Soviet Union			
			agricultural products	Soviet Exports
	total	% of	grain	to U.S.
Year	$millions	total	(million tons)	$millions
1972	638	79	7.3	96
1973	1,415	77	14.3	220
1974	957	49	3.4	350
1975	2,087	62	7.6	254
1976	2,527	64	11.6	221
1977	1,857	64	6.9	234
1978	2,503	75	13.3	254

Sources: Central Intelligence Agency, Department of Commerce, and, for grain data, David N. Balaam and Michael J. Carey, *Food Politics* (London: Allanhead, Osmun, 1981)

THE U.S.-SOVIET STRATEGIC ARMS RACE

	ICBMs		SLBMs		Bombers		Total Strategic Delivery Vehicles		Total Warheads		Total Megatons*	
	US	USSR	US	USSR	US	USSR	US	USSR	US	USSR	US	USSR
1990**	1,350	1,700	720	1,300	450	200	2,550	3,200	18,000	20,000	7,100	13,000
1985**	1,052	1,500	664	1,100	348	140	2,064	2,740	13,300	10,000	4,200	9,200
1982	1,052	1,400	632	950	348	140	2,032	2,490	11,000	8,000	4,100	7,100
1980	1,054	1,400	640	950	348	140	2,042	2,490	10,000	6,000	4,000	5,700
1978	1,054	1,400	656	810	348	140	2,058	2,350	9,800	5,200	3,800	5,400
1976	1,054	1,500	656	750	390	140	2,100	2,390	9,400	3,200	3,700	4,500
1974	1,054	1,600	656	640	470	140	2,180	2,380	8,400	2,400	3,800	4,200
1972	1,054	1,500	656	450	520	140	2,230	2,090	5,800	2,100	4,100	4,000
1970	1,054	1,300	656	240	520	140	2,230	1,680	3,900	1,800	4,300	3,100
1968	1,054	850	656	40	650	155	2,360	1,045	4,500	850	5,100	2,300
1966	1,054	250	592	30	750	155	2,396	435	5,000	550	5,600	1,200
1964	800	200	336	20	1,280	155	2,416	375	6,800	500	7,500	1,000
1962	80	40	144	20	1,650	155	1,874	290	7,400	400	8,000	800
1960	20	a few	32	15	1,650	130	1,702	150	6,500	300	7,200	600

*The figures shown are for "equivalent megatons," the most commonly used measure of aggregate explosive power. It is obtained by taking the square root of weapon yields above one megaton and the cube root of weapon yields below one megaton.

**Assumes no SALT Treaty limiting strategic offensive weapons. The numbers shown are extrapolations of official U.S. estimates provided in congressional testimony on the SALT II Treaty.

Source: Ground Zero, *Nuclear War: What's In It for You?* (New York: Pocket Books, 1982), p. 266.

Appendix 3

HIGHLIGHTS OF THE SALT II TREATY

The SALT II Treaty was signed in Vienna, Austria, on June 18, 1979, by President Jimmy Carter for the United States and President Leonid Brezhnev for the Soviet Union. The expiration date of the Treaty is December 31, 1985. The highlights of the Treaty and its Protocol are described below.

Numerical Limits on Strategic Systems

- 2400 limit on intercontinental ballistic missile (ICBM) launchers, submarine-launched ballistic missile (SLBM) launchers, heavy (intercontinental) bombers and air-to-surface ballistic missiles capable of a range in excess of 600 kilometers (ASBMs). Reduction in this aggregate to 2,250 beginning January 1, 1981, with completion by December 31, 1981.
- 1320 limit on MIRVed ICBM launchers, MIRVed SLBM launchers, MIRVed ASBMs and heavy bombers equipped with cruise missiles with ranges over 600 kilometers.
- 1200 limit on MIRVed ICBM launchers, MIRVed SLBM launchers and MIRVed ASBMs.
- 820 limit on MIRVed ICBM launchers.

Additional Limits on Ballistic Missiles

- Prohibition on constructing additional fixed ICBM launchers or relocating existing ones.
- Prohibition on converting launchers of "light" ICBMs (i.e. ICBMs with less than 3000 kilograms throw weight) to launchers of "heavy" ICBMs.

Additional Limits on Ballistic Missiles

- Prohibition on constructing additional fixed ICBM launchers or relocating existing ones.

- Prohibition on converting launchers of "light" ICBMs (i.e. ICBMs with less than 3000 kg throw weight) to launchers of "heavy" ICBMs.
- Ceiling on the "throw weight" and "launch weight" (total missile weight) of heavy ICBMs.
- Ban on mobile launchers of heavy ICBMs, heavy SLBMs and heavy ASBMs.
- Limit of one new type of ICBM on each side, which must be a "light" ICBM. New type is defined as any missile whose key parameters (throw weight, launch weight, etc.) differ by more than five percent from an existing type.

Limits on Numbers of Reentry Vehicles (Warheads)
- Freeze on the maximum number of reentry vehicles on existing types of ICBMs.
- No more than 10 reentry vehicles on the one new type ICBM permitted each side.

Limits on Airplanes
- Ceiling of 28 on number of long-range (i.e. over 600 km) cruise missiles per heavy bomber.
- Ceiling of 20 on number of long-range cruise missiles on existing heavy bombers.

Other Limits on Weapon Systems
- Ban on surface ship ballistic missile launchers, on systems to launch missiles from the seabeds or the beds of internal waterways, and on systems for delivery of nuclear weapons from earth orbit.

Verification
- To verify compliance with the Treaty, the parties will use intelligence-gathering capabilities known as national technical means (NTM). This includes photoreconnaissance satellites, intelligence collection ships, aircraft, etc.
- Ban on interference with national technical means of verification (e.g., shooting down or blinding satellites).
- Ban on deliberate concealment measures that impede NTM (e.g., placing concealment covers over ICBM silos).
- Ban on encrypting telemetry (radio signals transmitted from missiles being tested) needed for verification.

Protocol
- Ban on deployment and testing of mobile ICBM launchers.
- Ban on deployment and testing of ASBMs.
- Ban on deployment (but not testing) of ground-launched, submarine-launched and surface-ship-launched cruise missiles capable of a range in excess of 600 km.

Acknowledgments

We would like to express our appreciation to the following individuals, specialists in various Soviet and national security issues, who generously gave of their time as reviewers of those chapters of this book in their particular areas of expertise.

Madeleine Albright
Arthur J. Alexander
Vickie A. Babenko
Donald D. Barry
Barry Blechman
Donald R. Brower
Dan Caldwell
Michael Carey
Melvin Croan
William C. Cromwell
Robert V. Daniels
Basil Dmytryshyn
Charles M. Edmondson
Lori Esposito
John Erickson
David Finley
Sheila Fitzpatrick
Frederic J. Fleron
Robert O. Freedman
Mark Garrison
Dick Gripp
Steve Hadley
Arthur M. Hanhardt, Jr.
Bohdan Harasymiw
Ed Hewett
Paul Hollander
Franklyn D. Holzman
Holland Hunter
Robert E. Jones
Roger Kanet
John L. H. Keep

Donald R. Kelley
Ladis Kristoff
Robert Legvold
Martin Malia
Jessica Tuchman Mathews
Clark McFadden
Robert McNeal
Richard M. Mills
Matthew Nimetz
Joseph L. Nogee
Thomas Palm
Thomas Paulsen
John S. Reshetar, Jr.
Karl W. Ryavec
Norman Saul
Jerry Schecter
Donna Turkish Seifer
Robert Sharlet
Walter Slocombe
O. M. Smolansky
Howard Stoertz
Robert Stuart
Charles Timberlake
Elizabeth Kridl Valkenier
Rex Wade
Robert G. Wesson
Dennis Whelan
Fruim Yurevich
Donald S. Zagoria
Russell Zguta

529

Rome: the Enchanted
Our Sunday Vg Stot